MOVEMENTS THAT WIN

MOVEMENTS
THAT
WIN

PATTERNS OF RESISTANCE,
ECOLOGIES OF STRUGGLE

ARIC MCBAY

SEVEN STORIES PRESS
NEW YORK • OAKLAND • LONDON

Seven Stories Press
140 Watts Street
New York, NY 10013
www.sevenstories.com

College professors and high school and middle school teachers may order free examination copies of Seven Stories Press titles. Visit www.sevenstories.com/pg/resources-academics or email academic@sevenstories.com.

Library of Congress Cataloging-in-Publication Data is on file.

ISBN: 978-1-64421-508-1 (paperback)
ISBN: 978-1-64421-509-8 (ebook)

Printed in the USA.

9 8 7 6 5 4 3 2 1

Contents

Introduction

SHUT DOWN CANADA

Victories sustain our movements. Action inspires action.

That's true on the large scale, but also the personal.

In the fall and winter of 2019, I felt incredibly optimistic as a climate justice organizer. Youth climate organizing had exploded worldwide, inspired in part by Greta Thunberg's example. Groups like Extinction Rebellion were engaged in direct action and mass civil disobedience. Indigenous communities were making progress globally, defending their land and asserting their autonomy.

All this was driven by a sense of urgency, an understanding of the enormous stakes of the climate emergency. But there was also a strong feeling of momentum and possibility.

In late 2019, I was on tour for my book *Full Spectrum Resistance*, a two-volume exploration of how to build more effective movements. The timing of the book launch seemed fortuitous. I was giving organizing workshops multiple times a week, but the mobilization was much bigger than any person or group.

When I visited Vancouver to give action training that September, I joined a climate justice march of 100,000 people. The gathering was so gargantuan that once the front of the march left the rally point, it took more than an hour for the back of the march to start moving. It was glorious, empowering, hopeful.

The enormous numbers of people joining in—combined with a willingness to use direct action—meant that the movement had some of the key ingredients needed to succeed. Many organizers were new and still learning, but that's always the case when movements are growing.

It felt like only the beginning.

Inspired by the demand for action training, I started to write a new book with my friend and colleague Pamela Cross. It was meant to be relatively short so we could share it in a timely way. We called it *Direct Action Works: A legal handbook for civil disobedience and non-violent direct action in Canada*, and we worked on it through late 2019 and January 2020, as we gave training and support to different groups and movements.

At the same time as climate justice mobilization peaked, things were heating up in Wet'suwet'en territory on the west coast of so-called Canada.

The Wet'suwet'en, an Indigenous nation with strong cultural and political traditions, had been actively resisting the incursions of fossil fuel companies onto their land for more than a decade.

Like most Indigenous nations occupied by Canada, they suffered under the impositions of the Indian Act, which created a "band council" as a colonial political entity. These councils operate on reserves that are a tiny fraction of the original land base of the nations they are supposed to represent.

While on some reserves, band councils can express the community's will, they can also be easy for the Canadian state to manipulate. They are dependent on the federal government for funding and lack the ability to impose taxes to garner revenue from the enormous economic activity on their lands.

Because the Wet'suwet'en are located far to the northwest of colonial centers of power, they were among the last to be "contacted" by Canada, and their political and legal structures endure, particularly in the form of a group of Hereditary Chiefs who adhere to traditional Wet'suwet'en law and values.

"My grandmother was alive when the first Europeans came into our territory," Hereditary Chief Na'Moks told me. Cultural continuity, he explained, is one of the reasons that Wet'suwet'en resistance has been so enduring. "That's where we get it from. We never lost our culture. We've never lost our law."

Many band councils greenlit proposed pipelines; they were desperately underfunded, and the money that Canada should have been using to fund reparations and the wellbeing of Indigenous people was being used to subsidize the fossil fuel industry.

The Hereditary Chiefs, however, remained steadfast in their opposition to the pipeline. This was not an act of "civil disobedience"—it was, in fact, the upholding of Wet'suwet'en law. Chief Na'Moks summarized: "We are the land, and the land is us. But if we don't look after the land, we've got nothing to rely on for the future. Because our law also says that we don't own the land, we're only looking after it for our grandchildren."

"Our law comes from the land," he added. "It's land, air, water."

In 2010, a group of Wet'suwet'en people built a small village called Unist'ot'en on the planned route of multiple pipelines.

Those proposed pipelines would include Enbridge's twinned pipeline Northern Gateway and TC Energy's Coastal GasLink. Shortly after, Houston-based Kinder Morgan proposed the Trans Mountain Expansion Project, which would run far to the south. These pipelines were meant to allow fracked natural gas and oil from the tar sands to be brought to the West Coast for export abroad.*

---

* Fossil fuel companies at this point wanted to build pipelines from the tar sands in essentially every direction. A proposed pipeline running south through the US, Keystone XL, was canceled after years of opposition. A pipeline proposed to run across Canada to the Atlantic—Energy East—was likewise dropped after vigorous opposition.

The organizers at Unist'ot'en were pursuing several goals in synchrony. In an act of "re-occupation," they asserted sovereignty over their traditional territory, a much larger region than the small reserve lands recognized under the colonial Indian Act.

They also wanted Unist'ot'en as a rallying point to build a movement and as a healing center. They aimed to stop pipelines that directly threatened not only their *Yintah* ("land" in the Wet'suwet'en language) but also the planet. And they invited supporters from all over to come and help them build it.

"We drink out of all of our creeks and rivers up here," Chief Na'Moks told me. "They're not polluted, that's how hard we fight. People come here and they drink out of the river. And they cry because they can't do it at home. Some have never done it in their entire lives."

Despite living in a remote northern community—there was no mobile phone service at Unist'ot'en—Wet'suwet'en organizers have been incredibly good at reaching out to build enduring support networks. They've welcomed many activists as visitors to their territory who went home to continue organizing in solidarity.

"Everybody that comes, they just say it's life-changing," Chief Na'Moks explained. "You know, our law says: stand on the ground. Breathe the air. Drink the water. Eat the food, and you'll know who we are."

The campaign against Northern Gateway showed the persistence, intelligence, and creativity of Wet'suwet'en organizers. They engaged in smart direct action via Unist'ot'en, strategically located as a checkpoint to control access on remote roadways.

They also allied with many First Nations in the region, a coalition of which launched a legal challenge against the Northern Gateway pipelines, asserting that Enbridge and the government of Canada had failed to carry out the free, prior, and informed consent that was legally required to approve the pipeline.

They also worked with settler allies across Turtle Island and around the world to build awareness, stage disruptive protests, and pressure the governments and institutions (like the Royal Bank of Canada) that have funded pipeline projects.

This combination of direct action, organizing, and legal challenges worked. In 2016, Enbridge's pipeline was canceled.

This was a real win and important to remember and celebrate. It's one of many that front-line Indigenous communities have achieved.

Over the last decade, Indigenous communities in the so-called US and Canada have blocked fossil fuel projects that would have released 1.6 billion tonnes of carbon dioxide.[1] One point six billion tonnes is an enormous amount, so let's put that in perspective: if you are twenty years old, that's the equivalent of canceling out all the emissions released by every single car, truck, and motorcycle driven in Canada over your entire lifetime. I find that astounding.

The Wet'suwet'en struggle is enduring and powerful. It's also deeper and more nuanced than I have time to explore in detail here, combining long legal challenges and waves of organizing. I encourage you to watch the film *Yintah* (2024) about their land defense.

I've been a solidarity activist *and* a monthly donor for many years because the Wet'suwet'en struggle has had a far bigger measurable impact than big environmental NGOs, even though those established non-profits receive orders of magnitude more public support, money, and attention.

The Wet'suwet'en success at Unist'ot'en fundamentally undermined multiple fossil fuel companies.

In fact, by 2018, Indigenous activists were so effective that it was no longer profitable for Kinder Morgan to complete their proposed Trans Mountain expansion in so-called British Columbia, and they began to wind down activists to reduce "shareholder risk."

In a more democratic and sensible world, that would have

been the end of the proposed Trans Mountain expansion. The economics of the pipeline no longer made sense. Indeed, the oil industry should have become a fossil—renewable energy is now cheaper than fossil fuels worldwide.

Likewise, to meet its international obligations, Canada needed to stop increasing fossil fuel extraction and start phasing it out as fast as possible. More pipelines represented not only an expensive stranded asset but a fundamental threat to the future of life on Earth.

And yet, in the summer of 2018, the governing Liberals under Prime Minister Justin Trudeau decided that Canada would buy the Trans Mountain project from Kinder Morgan for $4.5 billion, using Canadian tax money to complete a pipeline deemed unprofitable for private industry.

Indigenous communities and settlers were outraged by the continued violations of Indigenous rights, and news reports made it increasingly clear that the purchase of the pipeline was a terrible decision from a financial perspective as well.* The cost of completing the pipeline had more than doubled to $12.6 billion by early 2020, and in the years that followed, it ballooned to a staggering $30.9 billion.

Meanwhile, government authorities and police were increasingly aggressive and violent toward the Wet'suwet'en. Though Enbridge's pipeline had been canceled, TC Energy was still attempting to complete its Coastal GasLink pipeline. Building on centuries of violence against Indigenous peoples, the Royal Canadian Mounted Police (RCMP) formed a new militarized force with the Orwellian name "Community-Industry Response Group."**

The RCMP increasingly used militarized police to ram-

---

* A year later, in summer of 2019, Canada's federal legislature declared a climate emergency. And yet, in a show of stunning hypocrisy, the governing Liberals continued to push the Trans Mountain project ahead.

** The RCMP was guided in their approach by former CIA chief David Petraeus—previously a general in charge of the US occupation of Afghanistan—who had left his government post in disgrace after leaking classified documents during an extra-marital affair.

page through Wet'suwet'en lands, attempting to terrorize land defenders at gunpoint to facilitate territorial access by Coastal GasLink workers. Instead of backing down, the Wet'suwet'en added another checkpoint, Gidimt'en Yintah Access, and continued to obstruct unwanted incursions on their territory.

In February 2020, however, Canada aggressively invaded Wet'suwet'en territory. Militarized police took days to smash their way through checkpoints and obstacles on the access road to Unist'ot'en.

The Wet'suwet'en called out for help and solidarity, and people across Turtle Island responded.

At Tyendinaga Mohawk Territory—long a place of vigorous Indigenous resistance to settler colonialism—members of the Mohawk Warriors society took over a major railroad crossing, shutting down cross-Canada rail traffic. (The Mohawks at Tyendinaga have a successful history of disruption and action—they'll show up again later in this book when we discuss the Richmond Dump.)

It's common in so-called Canada for railways to run through Indigenous communities. It's a form of environmental racism—affluent white communities don't want noisy, dangerous rail lines in their neighborhoods.

In solidarity with the Wet'suwet'en, Indigenous communities began their rail blockades, occupying the major railways from coast to coast. Canada's national networks were effectively shut down for the first time since they were built.

Settler organizers joined in, too. Pamela Cross and I released *Direct Action Works* online shortly after the police invasion began. It was downloaded more than a thousand times in the first few days; such was the hunger for direct action.

The motto of solidarity activists became "Shut Down Canada." We built on the cresting wave of climate justice organizing and youth energy to mobilize powerfully disruptive actions of all kinds. From rural communities to urban centers, activists blocked railways, highways, and international bridges.

This was a truly intersectional movement, combining Indigenous solidarity and a push for Indigenous sovereignty with an understanding of the threat posed by the climate emergency and colonial white supremacy.

The economic impact grew exponentially. The rail network blockades were stranding $425 million of freight each day and would soon cost the Canadian economy billions of dollars.[2] If the mobilization continued—and kept growing—the cost of resistance could soon be greater than the value of the pipeline.

This uprising was perhaps the most powerful expression of Indigenous resistance since the "Oka Crisis"—the Kanesatake Resistance in 1990. In terms of geographic span and economic impact, it was the biggest Indigenous movement in the history of Canada.

It was the most hopeful I'd felt in years—perhaps decades.

It was March of 2020.

CANADA: SHUT DOWN

"Shut Down Canada" had become the movement's motto. Then the pandemic arrived.

You know the rest. Canada and most of the world were shut down in a series of public health lockdowns.

It's difficult to predict what would have happened without the arrival of Covid. It would have been incredibly difficult for Canada to force the demonstrations to shut down.

Dedicated organizers were not going to back down, and the blockades were only proliferating. Violent repression of the demonstrations would have led to more infrastructure shutdowns.

The government could have tried mass arrests, SLAPP suits,

The blockade of a US-Canadian bridge on February 17, 2020; one of hundreds of direct actions using the slogan Shut Down Canada.

and conspiracy charges.* But that, too, might have backfired. The actions had strong support from enough people that repression would have mobilized more supporters.

Mass arrests might also have triggered a change in resistance tactics. If the aboveground organizing had been repressed, some organizers would have shifted to clandestine action. Openly organized blockades might have led to sabotage.

Canada has tens of thousands of kilometers of rail, power, and pipelines running through remote and rugged terrain. If nonviolent occupations had given way to campaigns of decentralized sabotage, it would have been nearly impossible for the government to stop.

In my opinion, if not for the arrival of Covid, the Canadian government would have been forced to negotiate with Indigenous peoples.**

Would the TransCanada pipeline have been canceled? It's difficult to say for certain. It's also possible that the magnitude of Indigenous solidarity actions could have shifted Indigenous-colonial relations into a new phase, advancing Indigenous sovereignty in the same way that the upheaval of the Kanesatake Resistance (Oka Crisis) facilitated the creation of the self-governing territory of Nunavut.

Instead, with the arrival of the pandemic, activism was stifled and submerged. The rail occupations and protests melted away as people stayed home, avoided mass gatherings, and tried to flatten the curve.

---

* A SLAPP suit, or Strategic Lawsuit Against Public Participation, is a frivolous lawsuit against public advocates or community groups meant to burden advocates with excessive legal costs and intimidate them into silence.
** Indeed, the federal Minister of Indigenous Services, Marc Miller, did go to meet with the Mohawks at Tyendinaga during their rail occupation. Shortly after, the Mohawks were offered a settlement for land claims that had dragged on more than a quarter century. And in 2023, Marc Miller returned to Tyendinaga again to commit $10 million for the construction of an Indigenous language and cultural center.

Mass Indigenous organizing entered a moment of quiet.* But not for long.

"CLAIM NO EASY VICTORIES"

Honesty is essential in the study of victory. Some organizations like to claim everything from the smallest rally as a victory. Others decry everything short of revolution as reformist or inadequate.

From my vantage as an organizer, neither approach is viable. We need victories—to achieve our goals and to encourage people. But we also need discernment. If everything is a victory, nothing is. True victories become hollow.

And yet, if we overlook imperfect or incomplete victories, we fail to grasp what these movements are in desperate need of. We neglect opportunities for learning. We lose a chance to cherish hard-won progress and ignore footholds we can use to advance our causes.

Activists and organizers must strike a difficult balance. We want to change the world for the better, but the obstacles can seem overwhelming. It's tempting to try to paper over those challenges and take a more cheerful approach.

That, in the viewpoint of many successful revolutionaries, would be a mistake.

"Hide nothing from the masses of our people," instructed Amílcar Cabral, the brilliant strategist who led Guinea-Bissau and Cape Verde to independence in the early 1970s.[3] "Mask no difficulties, mistakes, failures. Claim no easy victories."[4]

---

* It's important to note that the political and economic disruption of the pandemic did facilitate powerful organizing in many places. The interruption of business as usual, and the sense of broad social crisis, helped galvanize organizing around Black Lives Matter in the US in early 2020. And the free time created by economic shutdowns would increase activist availability for campaigns such as the old-growth forest defense at Fairy Creek, on so-called Vancouver Island.

Cabral believed deeply in honesty. His liberation organizing was based on a profound degree of personal and intellectual integrity. He believed in growth and exhorted revolutionaries to "dedicate themselves seriously to study, that they interest themselves in the things and problems of our daily life and struggle in their fundamental and essential aspect, and not simply in their appearance. Learn from life, learn from our people, learn from books, learn from the experience of others. Never stop learning."

For Cabral, these two ideas—honesty and learning—were inextricable. We must be honest about our mistakes and learn from them. We must see with clear eyes any deficiencies in our strategies to correct them. Ego and posturing obstruct that learning.

Cabral was an optimist. He didn't believe that honesty would lead to despair or defeatism because he believed that it *was* genuinely possible for his people to throw off their fascist Portuguese occupiers. Cabral believed that radical candor would illuminate a path to victory and liberation. That honesty is, ultimately, a source of hope.

And he was right.

Despite all the challenges we face, I share that optimism. That is why I wrote *Movements That Win*.

This book is a collection of stories grounded in real-world movements. I apply different kinds of political theory in a way that is directly relevant to the movement or struggle at hand and to making change in our communities.

Since we are discussing victories in the book, one of the first things we must do is differentiate between different *kinds* of victories.

For simplicity, let us identify three kinds of win: *decisive*, *shaping*, and *sustaining*.

Decisive victories achieve a desired outcome directly. In the

Wet'suwet'en struggle, the defeat of Enbridge's Northern Gateway pipeline was decisive. The project was canceled altogether—the outcome that Wet'suwet'en organizers and their allies had been fighting for.

Shaping victories are actions that make decisive wins easier; they change the *context* of a struggle to make other wins more likely. The massive rail blockades across Canada did not lead to the immediate cancellation of the Coastal GasLink pipeline. They did, however, rally enormous numbers of people and leverage powerful economic impacts that will shape Canada's approach to Indigenous struggles in a lasting way.

Sustaining victories make movement organizing easier because they are inspirations. The scale and strength of the Shut Down Canada demonstrations were uplifting for many. Their success also activated new streams of material support—like donations and supplies—along with new networks of allies and supporters.

It would have been amazing if 2020's mass mobilization in defense of the Wet'suwet'en had been a decisive win that directly stopped the Coastal GasLink pipeline. Covid made that impossible, but Shut Down Canada did offer many shaping and sustaining wins.

It shaped the future of the conflict by making it clear to Canada's federal government and the RCMP what would happen if they used open aggression against Indigenous communities.

Shut Down Canada also offered sustaining wins, brought people together, and expanded a sense of what was possible.

The movement's momentum was disrupted and dampened by the pandemic but did not vanish. Indeed, many of those same people and networks would be mobilized shortly afterward.

GRAVES AND STATUES

If you know anything about the history of colonialism in Canada, you probably know that beginning in the late 1800s, the Canadian government operated a national program of boarding schools.

In collaboration with various Christian churches, Canada stole generation after generation of Indigenous children from their families and forced them to live at so-called "Indian Residential Schools." These schools were conscious instruments of genocide, meant to isolate Indigenous children and deprive them of their languages, families, and their cultural heritage. Their goal, in the words of the program's architects, was "to kill the Indian in the child."[5]

It is impossible to enumerate here all the horrors inflicted upon the young people. Children were abused, starved, neglected, even murdered. Much of it was covered up for generations and not publicly admitted until the Truth and Reconciliation Commission investigated from 2008 to 2015. If you are not familiar with the reports issued by the commission, I encourage you to read them.[6]

Even those reports did not come close to exposing the whole truth, in part because some of the churches that administered the residential schools continue to hide records of their misdeeds.

I am a settler, not an Indigenous person. No one in *my* family was affected by this. But even writing about these schools in a general way fills my eyes with tears and enrages my heart. It's impossible for me to truly imagine what it feels like for my Indigenous friends and comrades, whose families continue to suffer the intergenerational effects of this trauma.

On May 28, 2021—just over a year into the pandemic—investigators announced that they had discovered the bodies of 200 children buried in unmarked graves on the grounds of the Kamloops Indian Residential School in British Columbia (BC).

Ground-penetrating radar confirmed the presence of the graves.

Further radar investigations—combined with archival research and interviews—later confirmed that the scale of child death at residential schools was even larger than previously known.

On June 4, 2021, 104 children's bodies were found in unmarked graves at the Brandon Indian Residential School in Manitoba. On June 24, 2021, it was announced that 751 bodies had been discovered near the Marieval Indian Residential School, Saskatchewan.

On June 30, 182 children's bodies were found near the Kootenay Island Residential School in BC. On July 8, 2021, another 160 bodies were found at Kuper Island Indian Industrial School, BC.

The investigations didn't stop there. Horrifying new announcements continued throughout the summer of 2021. The Indigenous resistance that the arrival of the pandemic had submerged burst back into public view with a powerful series of actions.

Those actions targeted, in part, the legacy of the people responsible for the residential schools. Chief among them was John A. Macdonald, Canada's first prime minister.

Canadians have long venerated Macdonald. Statues in his image litter the country. As the "Father of Confederation," Macdonald helped unify early Canadian colonies into provinces of a new country—a British-loyalist "nation" that could expand westward and compete with the United States to take over Indigenous territory.

Nowhere is Macdonald more strongly worshiped than Kingston, Ontario—the nearest city to me and the place where I've done much of my organizing in the last twenty years.

As the city's name might indicate, Kingston has a long tradition of deference to authority. Kingston is known for its military presence and history—European powers built early fortifications as a foothold for expansion into the Great Lakes and continental interior—and its prisons.

In Kingston, you can't throw a rock (or a can of red paint) without hitting *something* related to John A. Macdonald. He lived and worked as a lawyer in Kingston for years before starting his political career. When Macdonald was prime minister, Kingston briefly became the first capital of Canada (before being moved to Ottawa).

In Macdonald's honor, Kingston has installed statues and plaques all over town, and a major street and a school were named after him.

Macdonald was responsible for multiple atrocities. As leader of the ruling Conservative party, he expanded a railroad west that exploited and killed many Chinese and other immigrant workers. When Indigenous people stood up against mistreatment and the theft of their land during the North-West Rebellion, Macdonald used military force to put down their resistance and executed captured resisters—including Métis leader Louis Riel.

Macdonald put in place a genocidal policy of starvation against Indigenous people on the plains.[7] And finally, along with Egerton Ryerson, he created the system of residential schools that would kidnap more than 150,000 children in the century to follow.

By the summer of 2021, the remains of hundreds—and then thousands—of Indigenous children were being unearthed at former residential schools. Indigenous resistance mobilized on a massive scale, reacting to the horrors of the residential schools and the continuing hero worship of colonizers like Macdonald and Ryerson, who were responsible for those atrocities.

Their statues had long been targets of low-level discontent. In Kingston, a prominent statue of John A. Macdonald had been sprayed with blood-red paint in the middle of the night so many times that the city installed a surveillance camera to monitor that statue. That didn't stop the vandalism. A local pub named after Macdonald was the site of repeated protests that compelled the business to change its name.

In 2021, communities organized to assert themselves at a new level. Long-simmering resentments erupted into protests across Canada.

REVOLUTION OF THE HEART

In Kingston, the target of action was a massive statue of Macdonald flanked by cannons prominently located in City Park. City Park, located in a busy area between downtown Kingston and Queen's University, had historically been the site of a long-displaced Haudenosaunee village.

Professor Natasha Stirrett, a member of the Ermineskin Cree Nation, co-organized the action dubbed "Revolution of the Heart."

Professor Stirrett explained: "There was a lot of emotional charge around the discovery of the unmarked graves. Part of that was driven by grief, a lot of triggering of intergenerational trauma, a lot of rage, sadness. People were also experiencing isolation at home, so these factors really drove the emotional register of, you know, what was happening. There was a really thick atmosphere in Indigenous communities. That emotion really drove the need to take action around this for the community, to make a statement."

Stirrett and other organizers had advocated for the statue's removal in years past, including during a similar reckoning about Confederate statues in the United States. Still, that moment in summer 2021 provided special opportunities they wanted to seize.

On June 10, 2021, Stirrett and other organizers went to City Park, scaled the massive statue, and wrapped it in red cloth. They promised that they would not move until the statue was dismantled.

They also lit a sacred fire on the site, which was kept burning for the duration of the action.

"The sacred fire is not a campfire," Professor Stirrett explains. "It's a connection to the spirit world and to the ancestors. It's ceremony. It's opening up that portal between us and the ancestral world. It's an opportunity to have ceremony, you can make offerings of tobacco and cedar."

The context of the pandemic *boosted* the action in many ways. Stirrett explains: "There was a lot of capacity and organizing already happening around the pandemic. For example, Mutual Aid Katarokwi-Kingston had just emerged as an organizing group, so they had a bunch of like volunteer base.* They had a bunch of connections, they were organized, they had a communication system through Signal [the encrypted messaging app].

"It was a really good moment to make a move because of the emotional intensity and rage against what was happening around the unmarked graves, and the pandemic compounding that. Even though it was a very difficult moment, we were able to tap into that *drive* or that *need* for something to happen for change."

The location helped, too, Stirrett explains. "The pandemic really played to our favor, because we were in a public park and there were mandates about how many people could be together inside. And there was nothing to do. Everything was closed. So, people said, 'Oh well, I'll just go to the park to support this event because nothing else is happening.'

"People who normally would be distracted—they're going to play soccer or they're going to play a music gig so they don't have time to show up—all of a sudden, people had nothing *but* time."

Free time, however, isn't enough to overcome centuries of colonialism. Kingston had rejected past calls to remove the statue; at the beginning of the action, the city government was only willing to entertain changing the wording of the plaque on the statue.

---

* Mutual Aid Katarokwi-Kingston is a grassroots group rooted in anarchist traditions, which formed early in the pandemic to support people who needed to isolate due to Covid, or who were affected by the economic and social upheaval of that moment. They continue to do support and advocacy work in the community, including for unhoused people.

It was clear that convincing Kingston officials to remove the statue would not be easy. Stirrett recalls: "Even friends of mine said, 'They're never going to take it down. You're wasting your time.'

"You have to be stubborn and just *believe*. Dig your heels in and believe the impossible could be possible. We didn't necessarily have a clear vision of how to get there. But we had community, we had the capacity, we had the resources, the support."

In the first twenty-four hours, it wasn't clear exactly how much support Revolution of the Heart would get. "We were prepared to be there for months," Professor Stirrett told me—but that's a very long time. I was one of many people who supported the action by bringing supplies and equipment.

"It started to rain on the second day," Stirrett recalls. "We said, well, let's buckle down. I guess we're doing this. It was starting to rain, and you showed up with a tent. Those moments of kindness from the community kept the momentum going. It was grassroots-driven.

"When there was a need, people just came and filled it. Another tent showed up, and then some chairs showed up." Non-Indigenous solidarity activists helped fill whatever needs arose at the sacred fire. People with connections helped to get a key for a bathroom in the park that had previously been locked. All these factors gave Indigenous organizers the staying power they needed to endure.

Because of the public location, many people who came to the site didn't understand what was happening or why. They weren't aggressive, but their repetitious and sometimes ignorant questions could be exhausting for Indigenous organizers who were already experiencing a traumatic time. Settler allies set up an "info tent" a short distance from the sacred fire and took on some of the responsibility of having educational conversations with passersby.

Despite this support, it wasn't easy. "It was very intense every day, effectively because you were *on* twenty-four seven, the entire time. You were kind of in action mode. There were roller coasters of emotion from empowerment to fear." Some racists in the community would drive by and shout profanities at the activists, including at night. White supremacists put up racist graffiti near the site. One angry man became aggressive and threatened to come back with a gun. Community allies were on site—sometimes in large numbers—to maintain safety.

"But it was very joyful. We had a lot of community-oriented things. We'd have an impromptu music jam, a drumming group, teach-in, or dancing. Powerful imprinting experiences, for sure."

This way of taking up space was inviting community while ensuring authorities had no excuse to crack down on the site. Stirrett says: "Embracing people into the experience was key to success. It wasn't some kind of opposition to community. It was reaching out to community and saying 'we're in pain, we're angry, we're upset. This is why. Come learn about why. Come support us. Come participate. Come learn."

Stirrett and other organizers strove to keep a confident mood at the site. "It was nonviolent resistance. It was peaceful. Kids were there. It's easier [for authorities] to shut down what people perceive as some kind of threatening entity. But it wasn't that at all."

But police and city officials didn't know how to respond to this kind of firm, nonviolent action. "It was unprecedented in some ways. The city never had to deal with that before that kind of bold demonstration. They were kind of fearful."

As the organizers settled in, momentum grew, Professor Stirrett explains. "As we started gaining ground, we started gaining more capacity, and we had more resources. We were able to be bolder articulating the terms of our demands.

"We wanted *them* to take it down. We didn't want to be the ones that did it. They knew that if they didn't do it, someone else would."

That was a real possibility. The same week that the Revolution of the Heart action began, a group of demonstrators in Toronto targeted a statue of Egerton Ryerson, architect of the residential school system. The statue was in front of Ryerson University, which had been named in the colonizer's honor.

Demonstrators surrounded the statue of Ryerson, splattered it with red paint, then toppled it and decapitated it. The bronze head was later put on a pike at the 1492 Land Back Lane reclamation camp at Six Nations of the Grand River. The University wisely capitulated—instead of trying to restore the statue, they removed the pedestal. The entire institution was later renamed from Ryerson University to Toronto Metropolitan University.

The year before, a statue of Macdonald of Montreal—likewise a target of current vandalism—had been toppled and decapitated by demonstrators as part of a Defund the Police march.

Stirrett recalls: "Some people from the city had real emotional attachments to the statue, and they didn't want it to be destroyed, potentially."

Activists organized an intense advocacy campaign, calling and emailing city council members. Hundreds of community members lobbied their councillors for the immediate removal of the statue. The pressure on city authorities became intense, Stirrett explains: "Mostly because they didn't want us there for longer than need be. They were really quick to move because they'd seen what was growing there; they didn't know how to handle it, and they didn't want to deal with it."

Kingston's city council called an emergency meeting, and that broadcast immediately became the most-watched livestream in Kingston's municipal history. Many people spoke in favor of removing the statue. A few wanted to keep it.

Kingston officials eventually gave in to the public's will and voted to remove the statue. On June 18, it was removed by crane and put into "temporary storage," where it remains to this day.

Other statues were removed one after another. In Charlottetown, Prince Edward Island, a statue of Macdonald was removed less than twenty-four hours after Indigenous people began a vigil there. In Picton, Ontario, a statue of Macdonald was voluntarily removed by the city council.

In Hamilton, Ontario, city officials voted in July *not* to remove their status of Macdonald. In response, demonstrators toppled it themselves. The statue has not been replaced.

Statues of other colonizers were likewise removed. On July 1 (Canada Day), demonstrators in Winnipeg splattered a statue of Queen Victoria with red paint, toppled it, and threw the head into the Assiniboine River. In Victoria, BC, that same day, activists pulled down a statue of Captain James Cook and threw it into the sea.

These actions continued into 2022. In Vancouver, a statue of colonizer John Deighton had been splattered with red paint because, in 1870, Deighton had married a twelve-year-old Squamish girl named Quahail-ya. A petition for the statue's removal (signed by 23,000 people) had been ignored. During the annual memorial march for Missing and Murdered Indigenous Women and Girls, demonstrators pulled down the statue themselves.

Aside from the benefits of owning a battery-powered angle grinder, all this points to the power of radical flanking. Local movements against statues in other cities helped give organizers leverage to successfully pressure Kingston officials.

Professor Stirrett explains that, in addition to strong community pressure, Kingston officials were well aware of the overall mood and what was happening to colonial statues in other places. "They knew if they didn't take it down, someone else would. And they think that's really what drove the city to take it down, even though they didn't want to."

What did she learn from the action? "I've learned to trust the process," Stirrett told me. "I learned to never discount what could be possible. And I learned how effective direct action is. That it is a shortcut for what can normally take years."

The ten-day campaign to remove the statue was a powerful movement-building opportunity. It was also a genuine chance to develop a deeper understanding in our community of John A Macdonald's true history and the evils of colonialism.

The most common argument from people who wanted to keep the statue in place was that it was educational. *You can't erase history*, etc., etc. However, one thing that this campaign made clear was that the statute had no educational benefits whatsoever.

During their action, Revolution of the Heart became a beacon for settlers who had strong but confused feelings about John A. Macdonald. I spent many an hour speaking with people who would wander up to the site, and who sometimes felt very upset about things they had trouble articulating.

My conversations with other settlers made it very clear that—despite so many statues, events, and schools named to honor colonizers like Macdonald—most Canadians knew almost nothing about Canada's real history. And that wasn't accidental—that was Canada's educational system functioning as intended.

The sacred fire also offered an opportunity to speak honestly with people about the realities of Canada's colonial history. The demonstrations, rallies, and destruction of those statues created more genuine education than the presence of the statues ever had.

"It completely changed the narrative," says Professor Stirrett. "It was absolutely transformed."

"We had been challenging the narrative around John A. and his legacy for five, six, seven years prior to that. And people just didn't get it.

"After Revolution of the heart, the public discourse has vastly changed. It drastically shifted in a very short period of time. And

I think that's the power of direct action, right? People do direct action because it works. They do it because they don't have any other option.

"It was a moment where we just needed to take a stand and be like: 'You know what? This wasn't okay. This isn't okay. It's not okay to celebrate the murder of our children, or to have statues in the park that glorify this legacy.'"

Before the action, she explains, few people understood anything about what Macdonald actually did or how he treated Indigenous people. The action changed that. "A year later, I took a taxi down to the park. And the cab driver said 'Oh yeah, that's where the statue used to be. Yeah, that should have come down a long time ago.'

"He wouldn't have known anything about John A. or Indigenous people had that action not happened."

WHY STUDY VICTORIES?

I love to study movement victories. Study is, perhaps, too *dry* a word.

For those of us dedicated to social and political transformation, learning and understanding the principles behind success is a strategic necessity. Amílcar Cabral described it as a kind of duty.

But it's also a privilege, a joy, an opportunity, a chance to revel in resistance. Movement victories are not only instructive but also sources of inspiration and motivation.

Every victory is the fruit of work and struggle. The fruit of victory is sweet and can nourish and sustain us in difficult times. It can provide us with energy when we tire and the promise of moisture when our mouths are parched.

And each fruit contains seeds—the seeds of future struggle and victories. Within these stories, we see how success begets success, how a win on one continent inspires a movement on another.

I want to feast on victory, to scatter the seeds of victory far and wide. And in this historical moment, we must study success.

Climate change is here, filling our skies with smoke and battering our communities with heat waves, storms, and extreme weather.

War proliferates. Inequality grows. Democracies long undermined by corporate power are at risk of being swept away by fascism.

All this is likely going to get worse before it gets better. Most everyone can see that now. Public opinion surveys about the future are increasingly pessimistic—even bleak.

There is no shortage of horror in the world. Our news and social media feeds are a deluge of injustice and atrocity.

But that's not enough to motivate people. That's not enough to build movements.

The opposite is true: showing people horror *without* a credible call to action demobilizes people. It encourages them to withdraw into escapism, away from the collective action to private life. I would argue that's one *purpose* of the corporate news media in our society. Media that include both a call to action and a structural analysis of the problems we face—from long-running stalwarts like *Democracy Now!* to newcomers like the climate newsletter *HEATED*—are threats to the status quo and threats to those in power.

If we speak honestly about our society's wrongs and injustices, then it's incumbent on us as organizers to share ways that people can take action and succeed. Otherwise, we are undermining our work and our future.

Outrage by itself can achieve very little without collective action. And it's difficult to recruit when all you have to offer is bad news and failure.

This is not only my perspective. It's shared by the most experienced and capable organizers I've worked with. And it's a function of basic human psychology.

Humans have a negativity bias rooted in our evolutionary background. We are tuned to "overreact" to negative information and to be alert for threats while often dismissing good news.

Negative stories stick in our minds. A little negativity can have a significant and lasting impact by changing our thinking and behavior. Meanwhile, we often overlook positive stories altogether—or, when we do encounter them, we ignore their lessons.

That's particularly important for new activists who may not yet have enough organizing experience to balance out the negative.

There is also a genuine risk that a focus on defeats, horrors, and damage done puts us in a mode of mental defensiveness. This beleaguered scarcity mentality can lead to a narrowing of perspective that prevents us from imagining different futures and possibilities. Dealing with the same problems over and over can lead to many of the same cognitive and emotional challenges—like burnout—that people in caring professions face. And they can trap us in mental loops and unhelpful rumination, the wheel ruts of the mind.

The mental and emotional landscape of activism isn't only about "positivity" and "negativity"—it is also about trauma.

As organizers, we experience trauma often—either directly or vicariously. Trauma can provoke powerful, involuntary reactions: flee, freeze, fight, fawn.

"Flee" and "freeze" are especially demobilizing. (So is fawn, since it encourages us to give in to—even worship—those in power.)

Of these, only "fight" is a mobilizing reaction. Even that, though, has its limitations. Anger is a powerful emotion—perhaps the most powerful driver of change (equal to love)—and is an appropriate response to injustice.

But if not properly channeled, anger can also lead us to lash out at our allies, attack those who could be our friends, and dismiss or disparage people who have goals in common with us.

Indeed, that's become a stereotype of the left—a "circular firing squad" of people who spend more time criticizing each other than those in power or who spend more time criticizing others than taking action.

Musician and author Andre Henry observed this on social media after posting a hopeful story that attracted negative comments. In response, he reflected:

> Hope is the fuel of revolution. The problem is that hope depends on imagination and imagination depends on memory. And our memory is full of stories of Empire's power, resilience, and brutality rather than stories [of] our own victories.
>
> We don't know the countless stories of outnumbered, underresourced people who have sought freedom and found it—whether by direct confrontations with Empire, escape, building alternative communities, or other revolutionary strategies. Without a mind full of these memories, our imagination for change isn't as strong as it could be. . . .
>
> Sure. We need the sobering reality that we have no guarantees of revolutionary success. But emphasizing what could go wrong, pushing what has and can go well out the frame, *isn't* realistic. It's false, first off.
>
> It's negative. It's demoralizing. And it discourages people from action. And that's exactly what The Powers That Shouldn't Be want, is for you to be SO convinced of the inevitability of failure that you call off the revolution before it ever becomes a serious idea.
>
> Pessimism won't save us. Don't be Empire's mouthpiece.[8]

It's important to be able to give and take constructive feedback among organizers. But the organizers I work with know how hard it is to make change, and that tempers the kind of feedback they give and the way they deliver it.

The criticism that Andre Henry is talking about is reflexive and unconsidered. It's a kind of knee-jerk criticism that usually comes from people who aren't on the front lines, who aren't doing the hard daily work of political change and community organizing.

This doesn't mean it's wrong to criticize others or speak "negatively." Sometimes, criticism is an understandable response to issues or inequality that have gone on too long. Sometimes, negativity is a response to toxic positivity.

What people sometimes call "criticism" is actually condemnation masquerading as feedback. We can give feedback that weakens our movements or we can give feedback that strengthens them.

Negative feedback widens horizontal fractures in our movements. There is a reason that those in power dedicate resources to deepening movement fissures and divisions through infiltrators, online "sock puppets" and troll factories, and covert operations like COINTELPRO.*

That said, of course, most criticism doesn't come from agents of the state. It comes from within our own movements.[9]

So, when we give feedback on an action, especially in public, let's ask ourselves:

Will my words help encourage our allies? Will this help build more action? Will this strengthen our relationships and movements?

Am I calling people in or calling them out? Am I treating other people with empathy and care? Am I using the medium best suited to giving feedback?

---

* COINTELPRO was the FBI's secret Counter Intelligence Program, which the US government used in attempt to destroy social movements in the 1960s. Their tactics ranged from infiltration to phony communications to assassination. Although the program officially ended after being publicly exposed in 1971, the US and other governments have continued to use similar tactics to suppress movements.

Whenever possible, let's be gentle, kind, and constructive with one another. And let's not do the work of those in power for them.

All this helps build resiliency in our movements, groups, and relationships. It also helps us to recruit and retain new people.

But there's something more. As Andre Henry points out, there is a kind of hyper-criticism that leads to the constriction of memory and imagination.

A tendency to dismiss wins for their imperfections is part of a reflexive negativity that reduces what is possible. I've been part of subcultures where people seem to feel safer *judging* than actually *doing* things that might be criticized.

This manifests in many different ways on the left, particularly in the difficulty of recognizing, celebrating, and learning from victories.

When drafting this book, I asked many people to share stories of movement wins they thought were worth including.

This proved much more difficult than I expected. Many people offered a story or suggestions. But even more people could not think of a single victory.

No doubt, though, they could name many defeats, losses, and endemic problems.

This is not a personal failure. It results from human negativity bias, the difficult historical moment we live in, and the prevailing culture among progressive activists.

I wrote this book because I hope to shift the culture on the left to focus more on wins and what we can learn from them.

We *need* wins to celebrate, inspire, guide, and offer models for effective actions. For the activist, a victory isn't merely sentimental. It is a landmark, a tool, and a seed from which to grow more victories.

Victory stories help us expand our positive vision for the future. Studying victories can evoke "positive" feelings like hope, validation, and excitement while encouraging us to think in terms of constructive actions. What outcomes and social relationships do we want to build and nurture—versus the negative things we want to defund, demolish, or defend against?

The question I asked about each of the stories in this book was simple: *did they achieve what they set out to do?* Did they create some lasting material change in the world? Did they stop something harmful from happening? Did they make something beautiful, more equitable relationships? Or even both?

There are also plenty of shaping and sustaining victories within. And these didn't happen by accident. Often, these are intermediate goals or objectives that can be set intentionally to make more ambitious wins possible.

The best victories are transformative. They change how people relate to each other. They change what is possible—or what is perceived as possible. In their outcome, or how people work together, they manifest the world we are collectively hoping and struggling to create.

The Green Bans discussed in the next chapter are a perfect example of this, a set of intersectional cross-class alliances that had a lasting impact on Sydney, Australia's physical and political landscape. But even the examples we've already discussed, from the removal of colonial statues to the mass mobilization of Shut Down Canada, expanded what was previously considered possible.

WHY THESE STORIES?

I cast a wide net while choosing which victories to feature in this book, including stories from multiple continents and time periods.

At the same time, I aimed to keep the stories short to make them as accessible as possible. I want each account to be concise enough for a person to read easily in a single sitting.

Most of the victories described are modest. They aren't global

upheavals or country-spanning revolutions. Big, dramatic trans-
formations and revolutions are important. They are also rare and
unpredictable, and as a result they can make us feel that matters
are beyond our control and put us in a passive mode.

In the pages ahead, I showcase victories that feel attainable—
wins we can emulate.

Each story is followed by a brief analysis of why the campaign
or action won. In many cases, I also discuss a movement principle
at work or compare different groups in the same campaign.

I considered many options before settling on this set of case
studies. That said, all curation is, to some degree, a matter of taste. I
have chosen to err on the side of brevity rather than comprehensive-
ness. Absolutely nothing about this book is definitive or exhaustive.
My selection is shaped by my knowledge and movement connections in particular locations. We all have our limitations.[10]

Undoubtedly, one could create another volume on the same
theme with entirely different stories. Even many volumes.

That's what I find exciting about victories—that there are so
many ways for them to nourish one another and our movements.

PATTERNS OF RESISTANCE, ECOLOGIES OF STRUGGLE

There are patterns of successful movements that recur at different
times, in different places, and for different causes.

One could call them principles, too. But that might imply uni-
versality. These patterns are common, but they are not universal.
They are ways of solving problems. They are strategic, organizational, and conceptual tools.

If I need to fix something on our farm, I repeatedly rely on certain tools: a claw hammer, a socket wrench, a cordless drill, a pair
of pliers, and a tool belt to carry them all around.

I don't use any tool on every project, of course, but I couldn't build a house—or demolish one—without them. They are, collectively, essential for problem-solving. You don't always need any given tool—but if you don't have it when you *do* need it, you're in trouble.

Patterns of resistance are much the same. In any given campaign, I might not need to engage in civil disobedience and disruption. But if I reach a sticking point in a campaign that disruption could solve (as in Revolution of the Heart) and I don't have that tool, I might be completely screwed.

Some projects can still be completed with the "wrong" tools—if you are willing to put in the extra work and time. But some projects cannot. A hammer is not a wrench, no matter how hard you swing it.

Specific patterns are present throughout the book. I invite you to watch for them as you read, and when you reach the book's conclusion, you can compare the patterns you've observed with the ones I discuss.

Social movements, however, are not inanimate objects. They are living things, made of people and relationships, ideas and actions. Building a strong movement isn't just a matter of picking the right tool or joining the right group. Successful movements are *ecologies* of struggle in which many different organizations fulfill their own unique niche—whether big or small—and choose the tactics, strategies, and organizational structures that will allow them to have a strong impact while making the movement as a whole more effective.

As you read this book, I encourage you to watch for different *ecological* relationships between the groups and organizations profiled in each story. By ecological, I don't mean having to do with nature or the environment (though you'll find many of those examples). Instead, I mean the kinds of relationships that different groups have in their movement system, how they can sustain, support, or nurture one another.

Are some relationships *symbiotic*, in that two or more groups all benefit from working together? I see many examples of mutual benefit in these chapters, including the boycotters and direct actionists fighting against Shell Oil in chapter 4, and the Builders Labourers' Federation and its allies in chapter 1, the Green Bans.

Do you see relationships that are *commensal*, in that one group benefits from the presence of another? You might recognize this in the nuclear disarmament struggles profiled in chapter 5, in which the more militant Committee of 100 benefited from mass organizing done by the Campaign for Nuclear Disarmament.

Or are the relationships *parasitic* or *predatory*, in that one group benefits at the expense of another? Such harmful relationships are rare in this book. That's not because they don't exist (they are all too common), or because I chose to exclude them from this book (I didn't).

Rather, I think it's because I have emphasized *success* in these pages. Movements that win rely heavily on cooperation, mutual aid, and symbiosis. True collaboration gives any movement a tremendous boost, makes it much more likely to attain its goals. Movements made up of groups that harm one another, in contrast, suffer greatly and are less likely to prevail.

Diversity is also critical to ecologies of struggle, just as it is to natural ecologies and biomes. That kind of diversity includes what many people mean by the term: diversity of thought and opinion, gender, ethnic backgrounds, and so on. But it means diversity in the style of organization and action. Movements that win include big tent organizations with broad principles, as well as small organizations whose opinions and analysis are razor-sharp. Movements that use low-risk tactics like boycotts and petitions to mobilize end masse, but also high-risk tactics of disruption and direct action that allow a handful of people to make a big impact. Diverse movements offer a place for people from many

backgrounds, from many schools of thought, and so they ultimately become bigger and more powerful than groups based on
rigid ideological conformity.

Ecological monocultures—whether in movements or nature—
are brittle. They are highly vulnerable to stress, whether that's a
new form of repression or a new insect pest, and they can easily
collapse. They are prone to cycles of boom and bust, of fad and
fade.

Profound and transformative change demands sustained action
of the kind that can only be generated by rich ecologies of struggle.
It is diversity of thought and action that makes movements resil-
ient and adaptable, allowing them to grow, thrive, and ultimately
succeed.

A GENTLE WARNING

Before we proceed, let me offer a gentle warning

Movement success always brings backlash.

In the pages ahead, I intentionally avoid violent or gruesome
details. However, in some of these stories, people die. People are
murdered.

While I aim to be positive and focus on the beauty of what has
been achieved, this book is not intended to be "chicken soup for
the activist soul."

Victory without sacrifice is a rare thing. While I won't wallow
in atrocities, I won't shy away from the realities of repression.
Sometimes, we must take the bitter along with the sweet.

I could have trimmed out the tough parts or limited this collection of stories to ones where nothing truly terrible happened, but
that wouldn't have been honest or helpful.

We need the full story to:

★ *Prepare for hard times* and support each other when the going gets tough.

★ *Engage with repression as a group and protect our members* rather than leaving individuals to fend for themselves. An injury to one is an injury to all.

★ *Recognize that the risks of activism are different for different people* (because of privilege and inequality) and act accordingly by trying to reduce the risks to people who are marginalized or precarious while encouraging people of privilege to step out of their comfort zones.

★ *Put risks in perspective.* The risks of taking action are real, but they are ultimately smaller than the risks of inaction that could lead to catastrophic climate change or rampant authoritarianism.

★ *Recognize that we are part of a common humanity.* Making change is always hard. By understanding that the challenges of activism span decades and continents, we can develop more resilience and self-compassion in ourselves and our groups.

★ *Be grateful for the sacrifices others have made* to earn the rights and freedoms we have now (as opposed to whitewashed or sanitized histories that treat social progress as some kind of automatic or inevitable outcome). In other words, I'm guided in this book by Cabral's advice to *claim no easy victories.*

At the same time, I am ultimately driven by hope.

MY HOPES

I have suggested elsewhere that to become effective movement workers, people need a "radical triad" of at least three different ingredients: radicalizing experience, models for action, and a group with whom to learn and act.[11]

Unfortunately, our world now offers many radicalizing experiences of injustice—events that make it apparent that our societies need root-level (radical) transformative change. Radicalizing experiences are not in short supply.

As to models for action, well, one of the reasons I wrote this and many other books is to collect and share models for successful action.

That leaves the third ingredient: *a group*.

One of my hopes for this book is that you will not read it alone. Or, at least, that you will not read it *entirely* alone.

I've deliberately constructed this book to make this easier. Each story is written in accessible language without excess jargon. My hope is that people of many ages and backgrounds will enjoy this book.

I encourage you to read this with a friend, a book club, an action group, or some other small community with which you can build *shared* theories of change and common models for action.

You can read these stories in the order they appear, or jump forward to whatever story interests you.

After each victory studied, I include a brief analysis, expanding on why I think the activists won. These insights can be applied in our own work.

However, dear reader, you bring *your* knowledge, experience, and context. I encourage you to draw your own conclusions. Perhaps, before you turn the page to read my analysis at the end of each story, you might pause for a moment to consider for yourself: Why did this group succeed? Or do so with your friends, your comrades, your book club, your action group.

I have included a list of helpful questions at the end of this book that you can use to reflect on movements or provoke discussion.

You must bring some of your own insights and draw your own inferences in order to truly integrate the lessons of successful movements into your own life, work, and strategic vision.

I identify key factors that helped each specific movement to win, but more universal factors also appear again and again in many types of movements. I have discussed these in the final chapter to give you the chance to read through them first to identify those patterns for yourself. You are welcome, however, to jump to that chapter, read the patterns I see, and then return to the very first story. Either way, you can identify for yourself the patterns of success that are most relevant to your work.

In fact, I hope that you will sometimes disagree with the conclusions I have drawn! To be a student of resistance means that there is no one "true" way to make change. There are multiple valid paths and approaches. To grow as people and organizations, we must be willing to challenge "official" perspectives, find the viewpoints and tools best suited to our own contexts, and, when necessary, change our own minds.

ONE

The Green Bans

In the 1970s, Australian unions and neighborhood groups work together to fight gentrification and the destruction of urban green space. They use a powerful new tactic—the green ban—to stop billions of dollars of construction.

If I asked you to name two groups with a lot in common, you probably wouldn't say "construction unions" and "urban conservationists." Construction workers and conservationists are often at odds; conservationists want to prevent the destruction of heritage buildings and gentrified "urban renewal," while construction unions need those projects to proceed so they can have steady work. Right?

But it doesn't have to be that way. In the early 1970s in Sydney, Australia, *construction unions and community groups worked together* to preserve urban green spaces and prevent bulldozing of working-class neighborhoods.

Not only did they support each other, they developed a new and powerful tactic called the *green ban*, in which construction unions refused to work on projects that communities judged to be harmful. This was more than an abstract gesture of support—a green ban could stop a development project before a single shovelful of dirt was moved.

This tactic was not a one-off; between 1971 and 1974, there were forty-two separate green bans in Sydney. The union called each ban democratically in solidarity with community groups.

How did this unlikely alliance form? And what does it tell us about how to build strong movements to stop gentrification and development projects that harm our communities?

BACKGROUND

Sydney is the largest city in Australia. Between 1961 and 1971, the city grew rapidly from 2.2 million to 2.8 million people and hosted major projects like the construction of the famous Sydney Opera House.

In the 1970s, an economic boom in the sprawling city encouraged developers to pave over existing neighborhoods and parks.*

Capitalist speculation rather than human need fueled construction. Australian political science professor Verity Burgmann explains: "At one stage, there was ten million square feet of vacant office space in Sydney's business district, while people looking for their first homes or flats could find nothing."[12]

However, things were about to change thanks to a struggle at Kelly's Bush, the last undeveloped bushland area in the Sydney suburb of Hunter's Hill.

In 1971, a group of women in Hunter's Hill campaigned to prevent precious green space from being developed. The "Battlers for Kelly's Bush" had done everything they were supposed to do. They

---

* Historically, Sydney had dealt with population growth by sprawling out. Australia, like many former colonies, exists as a country because it stole huge amounts of land from Indigenous people. Land on the periphery of the city was cheap for developers in Sydney because it was stolen.

had approached each level of government, from the local council and the mayor to the premier of New South Wales. All those officials declined to intervene.

After every conventional tactic failed, the neighborhood group decided to do something unconventional. They approached a union, the New South Wales chapter of the Builders Labourers' Federation (NSW BLF).

This was an excellent idea. The New South Wales BLF was much more radical and inclusive in its outlook than most unions. For example, they strongly believed in racial justice: When a whites-only rugby team from apartheid South Africa visited Sydney, NSW BLF president Bob Pringle tried to stop the game by sawing the goalposts in half.

The BLF was feeling strong thanks to a 1970 strike in which they won improved wages and working conditions, boosting their sense of confidence and pride.[13]

The neighborhood group in Hunter's Hill convened a public meeting of 600 residents, and those residents formally asked the BLF to stop the development project at Kelly's Bush. In solidarity, BLF agreed to withhold all demolition and construction labor from the project.

This enraged project developer A. V. Jennings, who threatened to use non-union labor instead. Rather than back down, the BLF escalated and refused to work at *any* A. V. Jennings site, effectively shutting down multiple active construction projects. When BLF stopped construction of one Jennings' office buildings, they sent a note warning the boss: "If you attempt to build on Kelly's Bush, even if there is the loss of one tree, this half-completed building will remain so forever, as a monument to Kelly's Bush."[14]

A. V. Jennings backed down, and the development of Kelly's Bush was canceled. It remains a public reserve to this day.

That win alone would be a good story about solidarity and

community movements. But rather than the end of the story, Kelly's Bush was the beginning of a powerful new movement.

THE GREEN BANS MULTIPLY

Success spreads. After the victory at Kelly's Bush, many community groups and residents who had faced hostile developers allied with the New South Wales BLF to stop projects. The tactic became known as a "green ban" after the "black bans" used by Australian maritime unions to support Indonesian Independence after World War II. (See sidebar.)

The rapid pace of development in 1970s Sydney created a sense

An informational placard about the "Battlers for Kelly's Bush" which appears at the preserved Kelly's Bush Park today. (Stewart Watters, Creative Commons Atrribution 4.0 International License)

of urgency for everyone involved; quick action was needed to keep the bulldozers at bay.

The green bans—and the militant community-union alliances that enforced them—would save many neighborhoods, parks, and historic buildings. They saved the Royal Botanic Garden from being paved over and turned into a parking lot for the Sydney Opera House. In the neighborhood of The Rocks, they kept rent-controlled working-class housing from being turned into office towers.

Indeed, *New Matilda* magazine argues that the green bans "saved Sydney."

These green bans were powerful, but they required a diversity of tactics. It was not enough for the BLF union only to withdraw workers—developers could send in scab labor or armed goons to try to force construction to resume. *New Matilda* explains that "every ban had to be physically defended. Newspaper photos of the time show [Jack] Mundey, Joe Owens, Bob Pringle, and other union militants regularly being arrested and hauled off building sites by uniformed police."[15]

In some neighborhoods, up to eighty people were arrested at a time. Their success made defending these bans increasingly dangerous—even deadly.

> Union green bans saved The Rocks and Woolloomooloo from being turned into a forest of high-rise "executive suites"; they saved Glebe from being trifurcated by two major expressways; saved Centennial Park from being turned into a giant sporting complex; saved Victoria Street Kings Cross from destruction; saved Surry Hills from high rise; saved Ultimo from an expressway and saved the Opera House fig trees from becoming a car park. Individual buildings saved by green bans include the State Theatre, the

Pitt St Congregational Church, and the Colonial Mutual, National Mutual, and ANZ bank buildings in Martin Place. Bans also saved historic buildings in Bathurst, Wollongong, and Newcastle.[16]

WHY THE BUILDERS LABOURERS' FEDERATION?

Before we look at the explosive culmination of the green bans, let's ask a critical question: Why was the BLF so willing to collaborate on these radical, participatory, direct-action campaigns?

The leaders of the New South Wales BLF had a deep commitment to social justice and a broad perspective on the role of unions. They believed that in modern society, workers' movements "must engage in all industrial, political, social and moral struggles affecting the working people as a whole . . . Buildings which are required by the people should have priority over superfluous office buildings which benefit only the get-rich-quick developers, insurance companies, and banks."[17]

The NSW BLF also supported Aboriginal land rights and protected housing for Indigenous Australians in the community of Redfern. The union extended their direct action to fight homophobia in what some have called the world's first "pink ban."[18]

In 1973, a young man named Jeremy Fisher was expelled from Sydney's Macquarie University for being gay. Gay liberation activists approached the BLF for support, and the BLF put a construction ban on the campus. The administration soon backed down, and Jeremy Fisher returned to school.

The BLF was profoundly radical in both practice and analysis. It was effective at short-term disruption in its fights to improve working hours as it advanced to build a more fundamentally just society in the long term.

Other unions had also aspired to transformation. The Industrial

Workers of the World (IWW), for example, believed that every strike they held was building toward the One Big Strike that would permanently end capitalism. However, the IWW had trouble securing their short-term wins. The BLF, in contrast, used the green bans to apply their talent for short-term disruption to intermediate goals for social change while building a broader movement.

Members of the NSW BLF lived out their democratic beliefs. Union officials kept the same hours as workers, not the "bankers' hours" of more bureaucratic unions. They wore working people's clothes, not suits, and in contrast with more compliant unions, they had a policy of not eating meals with the bosses. While some leftist radicals in the labor movement (like Stalinists and Maoists) had a more top-down approach, the NSW BLF made decisions via direct democracy at mass meetings.[19]

Their analysis—reminiscent of later intersectional labor organizers like Judi Bari—was that "all work performed should be of a socially useful and of an ecologically benign nature."[20]

BLF leader Jack Mundey described a vision of the future that is even more relevant now than it was in the 1970s. Mundey declared: "Ecologists with a socialist perspective and socialists with an ecological perspective must form a coalition to tackle the wide-ranging problems relating to human survival . . . My dream and that . . . of millions . . . of others might then come true: a socialist world and an egalitarian body."[21]

REPRESSION

In 1974, Sydney's golden age of green bans came to an end. The two most prominent factors responsible were top-down crackdowns within the union hierarchy and violent repression by police and developers' hired goons and assassins.

The union crackdown came at the hands of Norm Gallagher, a

new national leader of the BLF. Gallagher was a self-described Maoist, but his actions in the union didn't match his radical rhetoric.[22]

Gallagher called the New South Wales branch of the BLF "over-zealous" and "crackpot" and said they went too far by holding up billions of dollars in construction work. He refused to meet with the membership, claiming that the BLF's support came from "sheilas and poofters"—derogatory Australian slang for women and gay people.[23]

Under pressure from the government of New South Wales, the authoritarian Gallagher expelled the local BLF leadership, black-listing them.

Then Gallagher set about dismantling the green bans and the grassroots relationships the BLF had built in Sydney. (Gallagher later spent time in prison for taking bribes from developers, though he was released on appeal.)

At the same time, police and developers worked together to try to intimidate and repress community movements that supported the green bans. Wealthy developer Frank Theeman was close with the government and "lent his home to the [ruling] NSW Liberal Party for glamorous fundraising parties."[24]

The culmination of resistance and repression happened in the working-class neighborhood of Victoria Street, where a green ban had endured for years. In 1973, a man named Arthur King, who was a leader of the residents' action group in Victoria Street, was kidnapped and threatened by thugs whom developer Frank Theeman allegedly hired. (Arthur King survived but moved out of the neighborhood after his traumatic kidnapping.)[25]

The police also worked with the developer's goons to carry out a mass eviction. One first-hand account describes merce-naries entering the Victoria Street neighborhood. "They sported sledgehammers, axes, and crow-bars. They shook hands with the police, and both groups moved towards the houses."[26] Together, the police and armed thugs attacked residents and demolished homes. Some residents barricaded themselves in and held strong through a multi-day siege.

The developer's crime gang set homes on fire in an attempt to drive residents out and accelerate the demolition of the neighborhood. At least one person died in those fires, a young Aboriginal woman whose name—in a display of systemic racism—was not even recorded in the newspapers.

As police and developers waged their campaign of terrorism, the BLF's green ban was canceled by the autocrat Gallagher. Thanks to activist and journalist Juanita Nielsen, residents were about to convince the Water Board Employees Union to institute their own ban.[27] But in 1975, Nielsen was kidnapped and murdered. Her killers were never found but are widely believed to have been hired by the developer, Frank Theeman.

Despite the horrific violence, neighborhood resistance persevered. Even after kidnappings, arsons, and murders, Frank Theeman was never able to complete the projects. Juanita Nielsen's house at 202 Victoria Street is still there; it's now a recognized heritage site.[28]

THE LEGACY

The cumulative impact of the green bans was enormous. Not only did they help inspire new alliances and environmental movements around the world, but they also had a substantial impact in Sydney. They stopped development projects worth over $19 billion (in 2021 USD).[29]

By the late 1970s, the economic boom had waned, and the building industry slowed. There was a change in government, and advocates pushed through new heritage and environmental planning legislation. The result? Many green ban victories have endured to the present day.

The model used in the green bans is powerful and very relevant in a time of rapid gentrification in cities around the world.

Of course, coalitions are easier to talk about than to build. Why could these neighborhood coalitions hold together despite violent repression, and what can we learn from them about building broad and effective alliances today? How can we cultivate healthy ecologies of struggle?

HOW TO BUILD A STRONG ALLIANCE

In *Full Spectrum Resistance*, I explore five key factors that make for successful alliances: ideological alignment and shared goals, prior social ties and bridge builders, crisis and tangible goals, political opportunity, and plentiful resources.

Were these factors in place for the green bans? Let's look briefly at each in turn:

Ideological alignment and shared goals. The different groups and communities behind the green bans clearly had shared goals, both short-term and long-term. They all wanted to defend their neighborhoods and green spaces to make Sydney a habitable and affordable city. They had the common values needed to work together—and while they weren't coming from the same backgrounds, they weren't narrow or rigid in their ideologies. Each group could see from different perspectives and understand how working together would benefit everyone.

Prior social ties and bridge builders. Green bans in working-class neighborhoods could rely on social ties between residents and construction workers. But the BLF and allied groups also had *bridge builders*—people with experience in different causes and different kinds of organizing who could connect and communicate with people who didn't have the same background. Bridge builders are crucial to alliances, and BLF organizers worked to support many movements, including struggles for Indigenous and gay rights that were not popularly supported at the time.

Crisis and tangible goals were significant factors behind the success of the green bans. Massive construction products were transforming Sydney. It was tangible to protect specific green spaces, heritage buildings, and working-class neighborhoods. The more concrete a goal—and the more imminent the threat—the easier for people from dissimilar backgrounds to put aside their differences and work together.

Political opportunity. The BLF provided a unique political opportunity because it brought together many different kinds of construction laborers into one union. In many places, construction workers were not unionized, or they were divided into very small and specific unions. The breadth and size of the BLF in New South Wales meant that it had the political heft needed to enforce green bans.

Plentiful resources. The threat of development in Sydney helped unify different communities, but the resources it offered also gave the union more latitude. Because there were so many construction projects underway and so much demand for construction labor—the BLF knew that they could shut down a project—even many projects—without losing all their income or going hungry. And previous wins by the union also put them in a more comfortable situation.[30]

An alliance doesn't need all these factors to be successful. But the more, the better. If we want to make collective action effective when a crisis does arrive, we must take time in advance to reach out to other groups and movements, building social ties.

This poster, promoting a gathering in May 1973, depicts the many intersectional causes supported by the Green Bans movement. It also features national BLF leader Norm Gallagher destroying that work. (Poster attributed to artist Margaret Grafton and the Darlinghurst Resident Action Group.)

If we can do that, we can move toward Jack Mundey's vision of "a socialist world with a human face, an ecological heart, and an egalitarian body."[31]

BLACK BANS AND INTERNATIONAL SOLIDARITY

The term "Black Ban" sounds vaguely racist to modern ears—but in the 1940s, it was a tactic of radical solidarity between Australian unions and the Indonesian independence movement.

What we now call Indonesia has been occupied by a series of colonizers. In the 1600s and 1700s, it was under corporate rule and occupied by the Dutch East India Company. After 1800, it was a colony of Holland. During World War II, Japan invaded and occupied it. Out of self-interest, the Japanese occupiers dismantled the Dutch governmental system but did not have time to create an enduring replacement before Japan's surrender at the end of WWII.

As that war ended, Indonesian independence groups pushed out foreign troops and worked to set up their own independent government—but the Dutch government refused to recognize an independent Indonesia. The Dutch government wanted to re-occupy the country and sent military personnel and materials via shipping hubs in Sydney, Australia.

In September 1945, Indonesian crew members on four Dutch vessels in Sydney harbor went on strike, warning that the cargo on their ships was going to be used to suppress the Indonesian independence movement.

In solidarity, the Waterside Workers' Federation of Australia refused to load or unload the Dutch ships and banned them from receiving supplies like fuel. Eventually, seventeen different trade unions upheld this ban on Dutch shipping.

You've heard of union organizers being "blacklisted" by employers. In return, the unions called the refusal a "black ban" on ships.

The black ban lasted more than four years. It was finally lifted in 1949 after the Dutch government officially recognized Indonesian independence.

GREEN BANS AND GREEN PARTIES

The struggle for Green Bans is probably the origin of the term "green" for environmental politics. German activist Petra Kelly visited Australia during the 1970s and saw the success of the green bans and the power of the movements that propelled them.

After returning to Germany, Kelly worked to form a new political party inspired in part by what she had seen. That party—the German Green Party—was officially founded in 1979. This was the first time that "green" was used in European politics, and the term soon spread around the world as green parties were founded in many countries, including back in Australia.[32]

TWO

Parcel C

BOSTON CHINATOWN
1993–1994

*In the 1990s, Boston's Chinatown had the highest density of any neigh-
borhood in the city and the smallest amount of green space. When a
medical institution tried to seize the last undeveloped lot for a new
parking garage, organizers fought back with a powerful coalition and
an alternate vision of a new community center.*

Boston's Chinatown has an area of forty-three acres but a population of 5,000 people.[33] In the 1990s—with only half an acre
of open space for the whole population—crowding and housing
shortages were severe problems.[34]

Both politics and geography were responsible. Chinatown is
sandwiched between two major highways, producing air pollution and safety hazards for residents. For much of the twentieth
century, Chinatown was also politically marginalized by structural
racism, language barriers, and a shortage of political organizations.
Many Chinatown residents in the 1990s were recent immigrants.
Over two-thirds of Chinatown residents spoke Chinese at home;
more than a quarter lived below the poverty line.[35]

Despite housing shortages, about one-third of Chinatown's
land had been taken over by two powerful medical institutions:

Tufts University Medical School and New England Medical Center.[36] Institutional land grabs had gone on for years without input from Chinatown residents. By 1993, only one undeveloped lot remained in Chinatown: *Parcel C.*

Boston had previously promised to turn Parcel C—adjacent to a daycare—into a community center. By 1993, without consulting the community, Boston cut a deal to sell Parcel C to Tufts New England Medical Center, who planned to turn the lot into a towering eight-story parking garage.

This backroom deal would have deprived Chinatown of a promised community center and created even more traffic, air pollution, and safety risks to neighborhood residents and children at the nearby daycare.

However, the people of Chinatown were done with business as usual; they decided to fight back to assert their community power and self-determination.

Andrew Leong, a lawyer, professor, and Chinatown organizer in Boston, writes: "Ultimately, the struggle to stop the proposed garage became more than a simple protest. It evolved into a sophisticated but impassioned grassroots movement in which residents, social service organizations, activists, and college students worked arm-in-arm with environmental groups, legal services lawyers, progressive scientists, and healthcare advocacy groups. Not only did the Chinatown community stop a garage, it developed methods and structures for community activism and grassroots organizing that will last well beyond this struggle."[37]

No successful movement emerges from a vacuum. The existence of the Chinese Progressive Association (CPA) would be essential to the success of the Parcel C campaign. I spoke with Lydia Lowe, one of the core campaign organizers and former Executive Director of the CPA.

"The Chinese Progressive Association was a grassroots organizing group started in the 1970s," Lowe told me. "It was a bit unique, started by younger activists who returned after being away for college." It was created when the Left was very active, and young organizers saw a need for a grassroots movement-building approach focused on the immigrant working class.

"It wasn't until the mid-eighties that it started to bear fruit," Lowe explains. In the 1980s, the CPA had a series of high-profile wins that raised their visibility and built momentum. They had landmark victories against police brutality—after police beat a Chinese man, the CPA organized a community campaign that got the assaulting officer suspended and eventually won a settlement. The CPA also organized for garment workers and won workers extended benefits and retention.

By 1993, they were in a strong position to advocate and agitate.

"It is in this context of a severe housing shortage, serious air pollution problems, chronic traffic congestion, a critical lack of open space, and the ever-present appetite of the medical institutions for land that one must view the struggle over Parcel C.

Parcel C was not just about one plot of land, or one environmental hazard. It was a reaction to history—a history in which powerful institutions and callous government agencies have continually mistreated a small and vulnerable community.

It represented a critical step in the struggle for Chinatown's survival. Even if the Chinatown community did not win the battle over Parcel C, it would send a message to Tufts and New England Medical Center—that the community could, and would, fight for its survival."[38]

—ANDREW LEONG

THE CAMPAIGN AND COALITION

Parcel C was designated a future community center in the Chinatown Community Plan of 1990. "The city had consulted the Chinatown community, and it was actually a pretty decent master plan," says Lowe. "Not really grassroots, but not bad."[39]

People were angry when the city cut a deal with Tufts New England Medical Center (TNEMC) to build an eight-story parking garage on that land. Because groundwork had been laid in organizing, the community response was prompt. Even before the first public hearing on the garage took place on June 10, 1993, Chinatown community advocates organized a 250-person protest in front of TNEMC and gathered 2,500 signatures on a petition against the parking garage.[40]

The CPA's history of community wins and two decades of outreach meant they could mobilize quickly. "We had a jump-start because we had a coalition," explains Lowe. Outreach and alliance-building were crucial to their campaign—as described in a brilliant organizing proposal, which can be read in the Parcel C archives at Northeastern University.

The Asian-American Resource Workshop (AARW) was a key partner in the campaign. "AARW was also a grassroots group founded in the 1970s, of young Asian American professionals, involved in Anti-Asian violence work," says Lowe. Many were engaged in post-graduate Asian American Studies work in the community. "AARW and CPA became the organizing core."

A third organizational component was a group of Asian American lawyers and law students, many of whom worked with Greater Boston Legal Services, which had an Asian outreach program.

Those coalition-building efforts were driven partly by a desire to build strong and diverse movements and partly by the practical demands of generating political power as the campaign progressed. Lowe explains: "We asked ourselves, 'What is it going to take to take to win?' We're demonstrating and demonstrating and getting media, but not getting anywhere."

They searched the city for allies with similar struggles. "Especially around redevelopment," says Lowe. "Especially communities of color that are disenfranchised or disempowered." Organizing committee members did the legwork needed to find potential allies, including attending other groups' meetings to build relationships.

Their coalition also worked to expand public awareness of environmental racism and to mobilize support from organizations, including the Sierra Club, the American Lung Association, the Environmental Diversity Forum, and the Conservation Law Foundation.[41] A group called Health Care for All, which organized around hospitals and community accountability, was also an important ally.

Demonstrators with English and Chinese signs at the New England Medical Centre in Boston Chinatown.

The organizing coalition didn't only reach outward; they also reached inward to engage members of the Chinatown community in an actual grassroots campaign. They held a series of general meetings on Parcel C, and—because language barriers had kept many community members from engaging with municipal politics—these meetings were conducted in both English and Cantonese. (The campaign's newsletter was likewise bilingual.) General meetings were promoted via phone calls, door-to-door leafleting, and notices in Chinese and English publications.

A woman speaks at a community meeting at on Parcel C, in front of bilingual posters showing injuries and other dangers caused by car traffic.

General meetings were critical, as Andrew Leong explains: "The Coalition used these meetings to update the Chinatown community about recent events in the Parcel C struggle, such as communications with [Tufts] New England Medical Center and the City, the success or failure of legal strategies, and the Coalition's future plans. The meetings were also an optimal time to encourage residents to be proactive. Coalition members would ask those attending the meetings to write letters, sign petitions, or help in preparing events."[42] Residents could also give the steering committee guidance on key issues by voting.

THE REFERENDUM

Initially, the campaign experimented with protest tactics and public advocacy. They met weekly to assess progress. "We tried different things at different times," explains Lydia, but the city largely ignored their protests and petitions, partly because the campaign was undermined by a handful of pro-business community leaders (the Chinatown Neighborhood Council) who supported the parking garage.

"We had to prove that the community was against it," says Lowe. Organizers decided to hold a community referendum, a process that would occupy their full attention for months. "It was a big logistical undertaking—ballots, monitoring, designing voting booths, deciding who gets to vote."

To ensure an objective referendum, the campaign engaged the American Friends Service Committee (a Quaker organization) to conduct the vote. "They're always going to monitor elections in the Third World," Lowe recalls thinking, "They can do it here!" The trust that partnership required emerged from long-term relationship-building. One of Lowe's first organizing experiences in high school had been anti-war activism with Quakers. The Coalition was also connected with an older Japanese-American man who worked at the American Friends Service Committee (AFSC).

"AFSC was the only organization that opposed World War II

A young woman casts her ballot in the community referendum on the future of Parcel C.

This bilingual banner appeared at many rallies and community events; for this event, the words "we won" have been quickly stencilled at the bottom corners in English and Cantonese.

internment camps," Lowe explains. When approached to run the referendum, "They were very keen and wanted to connect more with domestic struggles in communities of color."

Organizing the referendum took months of intense work and campaigning, leading up to a two-day vote. Andrew Leong writes: "On September 12 and 13, 1993, over 1,700 members of the Chinatown community voted on New England Medical Center's garage proposal. By an enormous margin of 1692 to 42, the community overwhelmingly rejected the hospital's garage. The Coalition was ecstatic. This proved once and for all that Chinatown did not want a garage on Parcel C. . . . no group of puppets could speak as strongly as the community had spoken in the referendum."[43]

AFTER THE REFERENDUM

Despite the definitive outcome of the referendum, the city did not capitulate. "We were still getting stonewalled by city, but [the] city was on the defensive," explained Lowe. "The referendum hadn't won the struggle."

With the support of allies and the community, the campaign explored new ways to escalate their struggle. They considered civil disobedience, but the development timeline still needed to be at the point where blocking bulldozers was an option.

Organizers decided to prepare a civil rights lawsuit. "It might not stand up in court," Lowe recalled, "but it will make the news and force them to deal with us." Again, the campaign kept up the momentum, seized the initiative, and experimented with new tactics with allies.

The campaign also used other legal mechanisms to stop or delay the project's construction. At the end of August 1993, with support from Greater Boston Legal Services and the Conservation Law Foundation, the Coalition presented Massachusetts with extensive evidence of the parking garage's environmental risks. They convinced Massachusetts to order a full environmental impact assessment.

That environmental impact assessment was released in February 1994. After reviewing it, the Coalition successfully argued to the state environmental agency that the report was incomplete and inadequate and needed to be translated into Chinese. Again, the Coalition was successful; the state ordered a supplemental report and a translation of key parts of the document.

Translation of the document into Chinese was a significant win that set a new precedent for linguistic accessibility in the state.

When fighting a development project, every delay is valuable. The Coalition made the most of the time won through legal delays by continuing to organize in the community. In August 1994, they held a Recreation Day convergence at Parcel C, temporarily taking control of the site. The Recreation Day was inspired by civil

A rally calling for a community centre on Parcel C; a mural on an adjacent building depicts scenes from Chinatown history and community organizing.

disobedience actions but was meant to be safer for community residents who did not have citizenship. The steering committee was worried that community members who were arrested without citizenship could potentially be deported.

The Coalition's youth team organized the day, which was "intended to regain the momentum and show what Parcel C could be, and how it could provide the desperately needed recreation space for children in Chinatown."[44]

At the same time—after a year-long community consultation and design process—the Coalition presented an alternative vision and a potential design for a community center on Parcel C.

By October 1994, City Hall was still refusing to meet with the Coalition. The Coalition's legal team had finished preparing their civil rights lawsuit, which would argue that the city had violated the Equal Protection Clause of the 14th Amendment and the Federal Fair Housing Act.

They planned to file the suit precisely so the civil rights lawsuit would hit the headlines on the same day as the US Conference of Mayors. This was meant to be an embarrassment for Boston's Mayor Thomas Menino. The Coalition informed City Hall of their intent to sue.

But before they could file their lawsuit, a journalist called to ask the Coalition: Are you aware the parking garage has just been canceled?

On October 21, 1994, a press release from the mayor stated that there would be no parking garage on Parcel C. TNEMC had withdrawn their application, and the mayor cut a deal with Chinese Consolidated Benevolent Association.

Andrew Leong recounts: "The Coalition was stunned. No one from the mayor's office had spoken to them about a settlement. No one had asked them to sit at the negotiation table or even give their input. Furthermore, the Benevolent Association was made up of the same people who sat on the Chinatown Neighborhood Council and had approved the hospital's garage proposal less than two years ago. The Coalition had been shut out, and the community sold out. It took a few days for the Coalition members to realize they had also won . . . It was amazing—a grassroots coalition of residents and organizations had stopped one of the most powerful institutions in Boston."[45]

VICTORY AND AFTERMATH

Some of the victories explored in this project take a troubling turn in the aftermath. There is often a backlash against success, or organizers have trouble maintaining momentum.

But that's not the case here. It's true that the ultimate victory—building a community center—took a rather long time and that the city did its best to cut grassroots organizers out of the discussion. However, the story of grassroots organizing in Boston's Chinatown is one of ongoing victories and progress.

"Before Parcel C, there was no pretense of democracy at all," says Lowe. "A 'neighborhood council' would just vote to support any development. Meetings were all English, no agenda, and meeting notices were buried in the back of the newspaper."

"After Parcel C, we forced the city to provide bilingual services and translation and interpretation. Community involvement in planning is now part of the city's public process," says Lowe. "These processes can be good when there is an engaged and organized community."

"A lot of the concessions we won are now policy," Lowe remarks, which doesn't mean that the community can take them for granted. "You have to be constantly vigilant. Even though we won these things, if people are lax about pushing for them, they won't always be there."

However, the series of community wins after Parcel C allowed the Chinese Progressive Association to grow and develop. "After every big win with CPA, there is always a wave of new activists engaged," Lowe says. CPA's reputation increased after Parcel C and its success and recruitment allowed CPA to become much more sophisticated and for residents to become active in the struggle.

I asked Lydia Lowe what she thought were the three critical factors in their success. She said, "an organized base, an existing grassroots organizing structure (or group), and a team of skilled professionals for legal research, alliance-building, and media work."

Something else that jumps out for me is that the Coalition had a positive vision for Parcel C. The campaign was not just a fight *against* something but also *for* a specific, tangible, attainable alternative.

That approach—combined with their relentless grassroots organizing—has transformed CPA's ability to increase Chinatown's political power through many different tactics, including voter organizing.

"Political clout makes a big difference!" says Lydia Lowe. "Nobody ever ignores our phone calls anymore."

MOVEMENT BUILDING AND INTERSECTIONALITY

"Intersectionality is baked into the ethos of the Chinese Progress Association," says Lydia Lowe. "CPA's founding principles were to fight the oppression of Chinese Americans and to build solidarity with other peoples' struggles.

"It was never just tenants' rights, or just anti-development, or just a worker rights organization. It always saw all of these things as part of the ways our people are oppressed. And part of the struggle for equality.

"Labor struggles have been a very strong current of CPA's work. The primary way that our grassroots leadership has developed has been more through the labor struggles than the development sites.

"The CPA Board is made up of all these community members who have been involved in different struggles. The garment workers, they're on the board. There are always people who came out of different labor struggles we've waged over the years. Some people out of tenant struggles are on the board. Some of the younger English-speaking activists who've gotten involved in different struggles, or through our youth program."

"Intersectionality is one of the strongest parts of the CPA's history and culture. I think we've understood that for decades."

THREE

504 Disability Sit-ins

UNITED STATES

1977

Disability rights activists stage a series of escalating direct actions culminating in four major building occupations across the United States. Backed by allies like the Black Panthers, the United Farm Workers, and queer organizations, the Bay Area sit-in lasted twenty-six days, winning their demands and paving the way for the Americans with Disabilities Act.

When we talk about "the civil rights movement" in the United States, that often means the struggle to end segregation and ensure basic rights for Black people and people of color.

The struggle against racial segregation happened in parallel with organizing by people with disabilities who fought to end their segregation and exclusion from public life.

In the 1950s, almost none of the accessibility measures we now see existed in many schools, institutions, and other public spaces. Wheelchair ramps were virtually unheard of, as were curb cuts and the gently sloping curves at intersections and crosswalks. Public doorways were narrow and nonautomatic; for wheelchair riders, it was physically impossible to access many spaces, from grocery stores to government buildings to universities.

And that's just mobility; braille on buttons, audible crosswalk signals, and closed-captioning on TV were also nonexistent.

This exclusion was not accidental. The prevailing attitude toward people with disabilities in the United States was that they should be pitied and medically cared for in a charitable manner but perhaps kept out of sight.

Before this struggle, organizer Kitty Cone explained: "People with disabilities didn't think the issues we faced in our daily lives were the product of prejudice and discrimination. Disability had been defined by the medical model of rehabilitation, charity, and paternalism. If I had thought about why I couldn't attend a university that was inaccessible, I would have said it was because I couldn't walk—it was my own personal problem."[46]

But things were going to change, and the 1950s provided new opportunities for people with disabilities to organize and take collective action. Struggles that frame disability not as a personal failing but as the result of social exclusion and systems of power require a collective, rather than individual, response.

The settlement of Black people in urban centers after World War II boosted the US civil rights movement, providing some of the critical mass for organizing, especially around desegregated access to schools (such as *Brown v. Board of Education*, 1954).

Something similar happened to the struggles of people with disabilities. In the 1950s, there were a *lot* of people with physical disabilities in the United States, in particular survivors of polio and military veterans of WWII and the Korean War. However, wheelchair riders were generally excluded from attending universities. (A UC Berkeley dean was infamously dismissive: "We've tried cripples before, and it didn't work.")[47]

Some successful court challenges began to change the situation; many people with significant mobility disabilities became students at the University of California at Berkeley, beginning with polio survivor Ed Roberts.

This created a critical mass of people who were able to organize and learn from each other. Wheelchair riders there formed a group called the "Rolling Quads."

They were able to agitate against the barriers that kept them from being fully engaged in society. Sometimes, those barriers are social or institutional, such as being kept out of post-secondary education. However, some barriers are physical—like curbs, which at intersections and crosswalks still had sharp corners impassable to wheelchairs.

The group advocated for curb cuts in Berkeley, but change was slow. As a result, they conducted a series of midnight "guerrilla" actions, pouring the concrete necessary to make curb cuts and ramps at several intersections in Berkeley. When the time came for the city council to vote on a curb-cut policy, the organizers packed the city council chambers with wheelchair riders.

This innovative combination of daytime advocacy and night-time direct action worked. In September 1971, the city officials voted to implement curb cuts across Berkeley.

It was a big win, and it was just the beginning.

THE REHABILITATION ACT OF 1973

Disability rights activists were not satisfied with municipal-scale action. They spent years struggling for federal legislation to protect the rights of people with disabilities across the country, modeled after civil rights legislation.

And finally, they achieved success with the passage of the Rehabilitation Act of 1973 (which was amended in 1974 to expand the definition of a "handicapped individual"). That act specifically banned discrimination against people with disabilities, especially relating to education, employment, and federal services.

The most important civil rights and accommodations in the act were contained in Section 504. While the language of that section was strong, borrowing from the Civil Rights Act of 1964, the exact implementation of Section 504 was left to the Department of Health, Education, and Welfare (HEW).

The Department of Health was supposed to sign regulations handling the specifics of this, and the rules were drafted with input from the disabled community.

Almost immediately, however, the government began to stall. President Nixon and his cronies believed the accessibility and accommodation measures required for integration would be too expensive. After Nixon resigned in disgrace, his successor, Gerald Ford, likewise failed to implement the regulations.

Jimmy Carter promised to implement Section 504 once he came into office at the beginning of 1977. But things would not prove so simple.

Organizer Judy Heumann recalled: "After President Carter became president and he appointed his Secretary of Health, Education, and Welfare, Secretary Califano, we found out that the regulations were, in fact, not going to be signed, as they were. That there was going to be another review of them, and that we were being told from people inside that the regulations were going to be watered down."[48]

The government claimed to be "studying" the regulations in preparation for "cosmetic" changes. However, information leaks suggested that the government was quietly dismantling the protections in Section 504.

Advocates prepared to escalate. Organizer Kitty Cone recounted that the American Coalition of Citizens with Disabilities, "realizing our civil rights protections were being gutted, demanded HEW issue the regulations unchanged by April 4, or action would occur. They called for sit-ins at eight HEW regional headquarters on April 5th if HEW didn't comply."[49]

"I think this was brilliant," Cone added, "because rather than waiting until watered-down regulations were issued publicly and then responding, issue by issue, this meant the government would have to respond to the demonstrators."

Indeed, seizing the initiative would be a great strategic decision, and a way to push through the delays and inaction of three successive federal administrations.

THE SIT-INS

April 4, 1977 came and went. The Department of Health and Secretary Joseph Califano had not put the Section 504 regulations into effect—regulations which had already been drafted, and which merely needed to be signed in their original form.

On April 5, disability activists kept their promise of action. They held rallies near HEW offices in eight different cities: Atlanta, Boston, Chicago, Denver, Los Angeles, New York, Philadelphia, and San Francisco.

The sit-in at the San Francisco Federal Building didn't begin dramatically. Instead, organizers including Kitty Cone and Judy Heumann used surprise and kept the details secret, entering the building after a rally to meet with HEW regional director Joe Maldonado.

Mary Lou Breslin recounted that there were no guards and no security response when demonstrators initially entered the building: "Pretty soon we had just entered [Maldonado's] personal office, and we began using the telephone and making phone calls," settling in. But again, no one tried to force them out, in part because of ableist preconceptions about the demonstrators. "I'm sure that whoever was there thought we were completely benign and didn't take the whole thing seriously."[50]

The government's underestimation of activists allowed organizers to establish a foothold and mobilize others to join the occupation.

The San Francisco sit-in began with approximately seventy-five people. That number quickly doubled, causing the government to bar the doors to new participants. Supporters rallied outside the building chanting, "Sign or resign!" Activists in San Francisco staged the largest sit-in; news coverage at the time reported about forty people in Washington, and seven in New York.[51]

Ce-Ce Weeks, executive director of the Easy Does It Emergency Services program in Berkeley, California, said in a TV interview during the occupation: "It's the first really militant thing that disabled people have ever done. We feel like we're building a real social movement. We want people to listen to us. We have tried negotiations. They do not work. At this point, we are nonnegotiable. We want those regulations signed."

A POWERFUL FULL-SPECTRUM COALITION

Lengthy sit-ins are intrinsically difficult. They are especially difficult when people with disabilities are occupying a building that is not accessible and lacks accessible washrooms and other amenities. Most Section 504 sit-ins were brief, lasting a day or so before being forced out.

But the San Francisco sit-in endured for weeks, thanks, in part, to the coalition built by activists like Judy Heumann, Kitty Cone, and others. Those organizers had been active in the civil rights movement and other struggles for justice. They had spent years strengthening relationships among potential allies and built a powerful coalition to back the sit-in and campaign. Many organizations were involved:

* Black Panther Party members participated in the sit-in, provided hot dinners every night during the action, and promoted and covered the struggle in their newspaper.

* The Gay Men's Butterfly Brigade, which formed to patrol the streets to stop homophobic violence, successfully brought walkie-talkies into the San Francisco federal building during the occupation.

* Glide Memorial Church, known for its early radical support of gay marriage and other social struggles, supplied food and other resources.

* Delancey Street, a grassroots rehab organization, brought breakfast to the sit-in each day.

* Mission Rebels, a Chicano group, provided food and support.

* Unions, including the United Farm Workers and the International Association of Machinists.

Organizers of the 504 sit-in framed the action as a logical extension of other struggles. Organizer Kitty Cone explained: "At every moment, we felt ourselves the descendants of the civil rights movement of the '60s. We learned about sit-ins from the civil rights movement, we sang freedom songs to keep up morale, and consciously showed the connection between the two movements. We always drew the parallels. About public transportation we said we can't even get on the back of the bus."[52]

For the Black Panthers, the sit-in made perfect sense in the context of their struggles around health (especially sickle cell anemia) and access to health care and other services. 504 organizers explicitly called their denial of civil rights a form of segregation, and HEW officials even used the words "separate but equal" to refer to the status of people with disabilities.

Cross-organizational solidarity created a broad understanding of the shared social movement goals intersecting at the 504 sit-in. Kitty Cone explained: "The composition of the sit-in represented the spectrum of the disability community with participation from people with a wide variety of disabilities, from different racial, social, and economic backgrounds, and ages from adults to kids with disabilities and their parents."[53]

This diverse cross-pollination made them stronger and impossible to get rid of. While sit-ins in other cities were short-lived, the government was unable to dislodge the large and well-organized Bay Area coalition. They had built a powerful and diverse ecology of struggle.

However, even this strong support did not make the occupation easy—far from it. To gain the element of surprise, many sit-in participants brought little more than a toothbrush and some medication to the action. Government and law enforcement would try to isolate the sit-in participants. Winning required creativity and inventiveness.

LOGISTICS AND COMMUNICATION

There were few amenities in the offices on the occupied fourth floor of the San Francisco Federal Building. Within a few days, the government turned off hot water and disconnected most phone lines. Police barred people from coming and going, forcing the occupiers to improvise.

To communicate with limited phone access, deaf participants went to fourth-floor windows and used sign language to exchange messages with interpreters outside.[54]

The FBI tried to prevent deliveries of food and supplies. However, groups like the Black Panthers, which had a long history of defying police and armed self-defense, refused to obey FBI orders to stop.

Since they didn't have a refrigerator to store sensitive medications, the occupiers built a makeshift refrigerator out of an air conditioner.[55] They even installed makeshift hand-showers in the sink, which officials tried to remove.[56]

Occupiers helped each other based on their abilities. It's reported that sighted quadriplegic occupiers read printed materials to blind occupiers, while blind activists helped their quadriplegic companions with tasks requiring more hand dexterity.

The coalition was also able to mobilize support from local politicians. For example, fourteen days into the sit-in, San Francisco's mayor, chief administrator, and the director of SF General Hospital arrived with a truckload of supplies, including towels and medicine. The governor of California also eventually endorsed the struggle.

ORGANIZATION AND DECISION-MAKING

These capacities were developed through planning, which in the Bay Area took place through the Emergency 504 Coalition. Kitty Cone recounted: "We set up committees to take on different tasks such as rally speakers, media, fund-raising, medics, monitors, publicity, and outreach." The outreach committee was especially successful in building a coalition.

Committees also continued during the occupation, Cone explained. "The media committee met regularly to review the coverage and discuss how to make our purpose more clear, how to use the press to get particular issues across. It directed reporters to appropriate spokespeople, called news conferences, and so on."[57]

One of the reasons the campaign was so powerful was because the organizers framed their demands in a specific and tangible way. Annie Rosewater explained that signing the regulations would make a difference for 35 million people with disabilities:

It would mean the children who have now been educated, if at all, in buildings far from their non disabled peers, would be able to go to school like normal children. It would mean that lots of adults, who now can't get into buildings, children who can't get into buildings, would be able to because building would have to change. No more stairs, no more toilets without ramps or open stalls. No more places where people who are deaf can't pick up telephones and understand what's happening at the other end. It would mean that people can take public transportation, get housing. People's attitudes would start changing because now they would understand that people with disabilities also have civil rights.[58]

The participants were a diverse group in terms of age and ethnic background. Women—including queer women—were especially active as leaders. But day-to-day decision-making was based on consensus. As Cone recalls: "All the participants met daily to make tactical decisions. These were flowing, creative meetings, but they often went on for hours, which meant very little sleep. But they were important in developing consensus and arriving at a course of action."[59]

Corbett O'Toole explained:

I think that for me what was really significant was that we were this very diverse group of people; many of whom didn't know each other. A whole bunch of people saw the demonstration on TV and just showed up and moved into the building with us.

It was parents with disabled kids who traditionally were not encouraged to know disabled adults. It was deaf adults; it was people with blindness; it was people with physical disabilities; it was this wild and diverse and divergent community of people.

And I think what was really striking was a couple of things. One is the way we made decisions, which was just sat around and talked about stuff and made decisions that way, which really freaked out the FBI, because they kept trying to say, "Where's your leader! We want to take them away!"

And so they were sort of very flipped out that we just sort of were able to evolve, and discuss, and just trust each other that we were going . . . that the work would get done and that we could made decisions in this sort of . . . sort of structured, collective way, where everybody got listened to, but we really sort of decided things by consensus.

So, that kind of legacy, that taught me that the sit-in, 504 Sit-in taught me that just sitting around as a group and listening to each other and coming to consensus about whatever we needed . . . that was important to us and moving on what we all felt ready to move on, and ignore what we all felt ready to ignore, was powerful social change.[60]

FURTHER ESCALATION

The sit-in was powerful, but sit-ins are resource-intensive and difficult to sustain. Cone recounted that "the conditions were physically gruelling, sleeping sometimes three or four hours a night on the floor and everyone was under stress about their families, jobs, our health, the fact that we were all filthy, and so on."[61] Some reported the spread of lice due to close quarters and a lack of bathing facilities.

After about two weeks, it looked like the federal government might try to wait out the sit-in. While a hundred activists were sleeping on the floor of an office building, Secretary Califano was sleeping comfortably in his bed in a fancy house in a wealthy suburb.

Activists then decided to send a contingent to Washington, DC. The International Association of Machinists (IAM) helped raise money to fly twenty-five representatives from the sit-in to the nation's capital. Once they arrived, members of IAM rented a U-Haul with an equipment lift to transport wheelchair riders since no wheelchair-accessible buses were available. IAM also hosted 504 organizers at union headquarters to provide them with amenities like phones and photocopiers.[62]

But their first stop in Washington was a midnight visit to the home of Joseph A. Califano Jr., head of HEW, where they held a candlelight vigil until dawn. To the obvious horror of Califano and his family, this garnered a lot of negative attention, particularly from Califano's wealthy neighbors.*

The activists organized meetings, lobbying events, and protests in the Washington area. When they arrived at HEW headquarters to meet with Secretary Califano, they found the building doors barred and guarded by police. Wheelchair riders, including Kitty Cone, tried to push through without success. Government officials were likely fearful that a new sit-in might begin at the Department of Health headquarters.

The trip to Washington helped to build pressure and media attention. It also made it clear that the Bay Area sit-in was not running out of steam but instead had become the epicenter of a growing movement. In Washington, Califano was dogged by protestors.

On April 28, 1977, the twenty-fourth day of the sit-in, the gov-

---

* They smartly focused their efforts on particular officials, and even showed up at Jimmy Carter's church. This followed Saul Alinsky's advice to "freeze it, personalize it, polarize it."

ernment gave in and signed the original version of the Section 504 regulations. Victory!*

WHAT NEXT?

Kitty Cone says the sit-in "ushered in an era of disability activism, empowerment, and legislative victories."[63] Their success prepared the way for the more expansive Americans with Disabilities Act (signed into law in 1990).

That continued momentum was sustained by a new mutual understanding developed through collective action and bridge-builders.

For Corbett O'Toole, director of the Disabled Women's Alliance, that meant building relationships and solidarity to overcome the racist messages she'd been bombarded with as a white person. "By far the most critical gift given us by our allies was the Black Panthers' commitment to feed each protester in the building one hot meal every day . . . I was a white girl from Boston who'd been carefully taught that all African American males were necessarily/ of necessity my enemy. But I understood promises to support each others' struggles."[64]

The Black Panthers, conversely, expanded their struggle for Black people to include new allies. In a speech at the post-occupation victory rally, BPP leader Ericka Huggins used the N-word in a reclaimed, transformative way to include all kinds of marginalized people: "I've been thinking since I've been here this morning that the United States has always had its niggers. And they come in all sizes, shapes, colors, classes, and disabilities. The signing of 504, this demonstration, this sit-in, this beautiful thing that has happened these past few weeks, is all to say that the niggers are going to be set free."[65]

---

* The sit-in continued until April 30, its twenty-sixth day, so that occupiers could confirm that the regulations had been signed in their preferred form, and so that activists who had gone to Washington could return for a collective victory rally.

Even the media, which had at first been hesitant to report on the sit-in, developed a deeper understanding of the importance of direct action. Reporter Evan White, who accompanied activists on their journey to Washington, concluded: "I think that's the only way real change is made, I mean, little revolutions."[66]

They achieved the goal that Kitty Cone described: "We wanted to get the American public to understand that they shouldn't be thinking of us as objects of charity or pity" but instead as a powerful force that could participate in society.[67]

Recall what Cone had said about her attitude before the campaign: "If I thought about why I couldn't attend a university that was inaccessible, I would have said it was because I couldn't walk, my own personal problem."[68]

Collective action and collective struggle changed all that for Cone:

> For the first time, we had concrete federal civil rights protection. We had shown ourselves and the country through network TV that we, the most hidden, impoverished, pitied group of people in the nation were capable of waging a deadly serious struggle that brought about profound social change. The sit-in was a truly transforming experience, the likes of which most of us had never seen before or ever saw again. Those of us with disabilities were imbued with a new sense of pride, strength, community and confidence. For the first time, many of us felt proud of who we were. And we understood that our isolation and segregation stemmed from societal policy, not from some personal defects on our part and our experiences with segregation and discrimination were not just our own personal problems.[69]

As Cone concluded:

> The thing I remember the most is our victory march out of the building into a rally. And everyone's feeling a total empowerment because we were a group of people who society had viewed as the weak, the vulnerable, without any real resource to power. And here, we had won this tremendous victory. You heard it all throughout that day. People were saying for the first times in their lives, or for the first times since they had become disabled they felt proud of themselves. You know, "I'm disabled and I'm beautiful!" You know, that kind of thing. You know, victory is a very wonderful thing.[70]

VICTORY FACTORS

The success of the 504 campaign had all the elements of full-spectrum resistance. Organizers deliberately reached out to build alliances with other groups for support and resources, and they helped those movements to develop a deeper understanding of how disability rights affected all kinds of people. They employed diverse tactics from legal efforts to direct action, using them in a complementary way to build the strength of their campaign. This wide-ranging support made it difficult for the government to use repressive tactics against 504 organizers.

They also developed critical logistics and communications capacities that allowed them to sustain the Bay Area sit-in for nearly four weeks and send organizers across the country to Washington, D.C. Their recruitment skills were strong, and their intelligence-gathering in advance of the sit-in made it clear to organizers that the regulations were being secretly watered-down, and that urgent action was needed.

Lastly, their willingness to escalate, tactical insights, and strategic capacity were truly impressive. The sit-ins used nearly all the tactical principles that make direct action succeed:

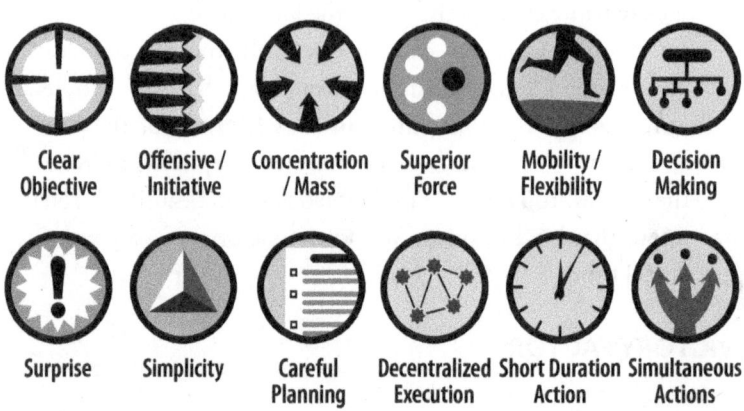

Clear Objective	Offensive / Initiative	Concentration / Mass	Superior Force	Mobility / Flexibility	Decision Making

Surprise	Simplicity	Careful Planning	Decentralized Execution	Short Duration Action	Simultaneous Actions

Organizers had a *clear objective* in passing specific regulations that had already been drafted. They took the *initiative* and went on the offensive by seizing government buildings instead of waiting for their rights to be whittled away. They used *concentration* of force by bringing hundreds of people to occupy the San Francisco federal building and *mobility/flexibility* by sending a group to Washington.

They achieved *coordination* during the sit-in through existing groups and lengthy consensus-based meetings.

The sit-ins relied on *surprise* to take over the offices, and although the sit-in strategy was ultimately *simple,* it required *careful planning* and logistical support.[71] While most of the sit-ins were short-lived, the nationwide effort was an example of *multiple actions* with *decentralized execution.*

The principle of *short-duration action* was perhaps the only principle not clearly applied during the lengthy San Francisco sit-in. While that particular action lasted a long time, there were many other short protests and rallies during that campaign that I didn't detail here. Besides, these tactical principles are options, not a checklist of requirements. Effective groups can ignore specific principles if they have the movement strength to compensate. The Bay Area sit-in overcame the challenges of long-duration action because of logistical support and an extremely dedicated group of participants and supporters.

FOUR

Brent Spar

THE NORTH SEA
1995

Shell wants to sink an enormous oil storage in the Atlantic Ocean. Greenpeace occupies it and wins thanks to direct action, boycotts, and mass nonviolent mobilization.

Fossil fuel companies often seem invincible.

They rank among the biggest, most powerful corporations on Earth. Entire economies have been reshaped to benefit them, and democratic governments have been subverted or overthrown to support them.[72]

The climate emergency has made fossil fuel companies the biggest threat to the future of humanity. But their vast resources—and the backing of police, militaries, and intelligence agencies—can make fossil fuel companies feel impossible to defeat.

But they have been defeated by activists before. Those hard-won victories can illuminate the deep principles behind effective resistance movements.

The story of Brent Spar shows us how to win seemingly impossible fights and how groups using many different tactics can cooperate to maximize their impact through full spectrum resistance.

BACKGROUND

In the early 1990s, you could barely pick up a newspaper without reading about the ozone hole, water pollution, or efforts to save the whales. "The environment" was a hot topic. At the 1992 Earth Summit in Rio de Janeiro, governments worldwide made declarations on forests, climate change, and biodiversity.

Governments and corporations filled the air with rhetoric about "sustainable development" and green technology. The UK and Shell oil corporation were particularly vocal while secretly planning a new campaign of ocean dumping that would endanger ocean life while subsidizing the fossil fuel industry.[73][74]

In the 1960s, oil companies built massive drilling rigs throughout the North Sea. These projects were hugely profitable for corporations like Shell and the governments of the UK and Norway. The North Sea contains Brent Field, one of the most productive oil fields ever; so much oil was exported that the price of "Brent crude" became the global standard. By the 1990s, Shell had become the most profitable company in the world.[75]

Extracting oil required drilling rigs and floating structures to store crude oil, which was later moved by tankers. One such structure was the Brent Spar, an oil storage buoy built in 1976.

The word "buoy" makes it sound like a small marker bobbing near a harbor. But the Brent Spar was huge; at 147 meters (nearly 500 feet) from top to bottom, it was three times the height of the Statue of Liberty.[76] Fully loaded, it weighed more than 64,000 tonnes (as much as 450 adult blue whales).

Extractive infrastructure in the North Sea was built quickly to capitalize on a "gold rush" of new underwater oil discoveries. Shell had no interest in maintaining old infrastructure—the billions of dollars from new drilling were what mattered.

In 1991, Shell abandoned the Brent Spar. As they talked about "sustainable development" in public, they planned secretly to dump old infrastructure by sinking it. This would amount to an enormous subsidy for the profit-driven company since Shell would not have to spend tens of millions of dollars on land-based recycling. Shell executives even expected to get a *tax rebate* for the cost of dumping the Spar at sea.[77] The UK Government quietly approved the sinking of Brent Spar in 1994, and media revealed the plan in February 1995.

Public response was muted, but environmentalists were alarmed. Greenpeace and other organizations had run campaigns against ocean dumping since the 1970s. They had recently succeeded in winning international bans on radioactive and industrial waste as part of the OSPAR Convention.[78] The Brent Spar's tanks contained toxic residue and sludge. Worse, Shell planned to unload the mess onto one of the world's most biodiverse seafloors.[79]

Shell hoped to set a precedent by dumping the Brent Spar. If Shell could normalize the practice, roughly 100 other oil and gas installations in the North Sea could be dumped in the same way.[80]

This would mean more pollution and an enormous subsidy to the fossil fuel industry in the form of externalized costs.

THE SEIZING OF THE SPAR

The response from Greenpeace was quick and somewhat frantic. Conservation organizations had been participating in a long series of often tedious international meetings about waste disposal; Shell's plan for the Brent Spar was an end run around the dumping restrictions being slowly and incrementally put in place. Greenpeace knew that *action* was necessary to prevent Shell from setting a new precedent.

Greenpeace organizer Chris Rose described the campaign in detail in his book *The Turning of the 'Spar*. Experienced maritime organizers, including captains and logisticians, suggested taking over the platform and occupying it. If they could hold it through the summer of 1995, winter weather would keep Shell from sinking it until at least the next spring.

It was a daunting proposition. Rose describes a recon video made during the planning of the action: "Shot from the wheelhouse of the Shetland fishing vessel *Starina*, whose crew pronounced it to be good weather for the time of year, our videographer's film showed occasional glimpses of a vast, rusty, red and yellow superstructure like the conning tower of the world's biggest and most surreal submarine. It was rising into view quite close, before vanishing behind fast-running mountains of grey sea . . . It frightened me just to look at it."[81]

Conditions in the North Sea were so harsh that Shell personnel used helicopters to get back and forth—even that was hazardous.[82]

Despite the danger, Greenpeace knew they had to seize the initiative. If they could occupy the Spar, they could decisively prevent dumping while pushing the issue into the public spotlight. They could change ocean dumping from an abstract and technical policy issue into something dramatic and tangible. Rose explained: "By getting there before Shell started moving the 'Spar, and stopping them, we [hoped] to challenge and expose those instincts and priorities in a way which was impossible in the mêlée of White Papers, green TV debates, and earnest reports on environmental auditing."[83]

After weeks of frenzied preparation, Greenpeace sent a team to take over and occupy the abandoned Spar on April 30, 1995.

Rose, who visited the occupation shortly after, described the eerie experience:

> The accommodation deck of the 'Spar was very cold and very damp. Abandoned for four years, it had the air of an oil refinery crossed with the *Marie Celeste*, with pin-up calen-

dars on the walls, lockers full of abandoned equipment, and, in the engineering deck, trashed workshops and wrecked control rooms which seemed to have been deliberately vandalised before Shell left them.

Below that, the 'Spar descended into a warren of cavernous interior voids, each filled either with dripping water and seawater that had entered from old injuries to the vast tanks, or cold stale air heavy with fractions of oil. Ladders and catwalks, huge pipes and dials twisted and turned through the 'Spar like the steel intestines of some vast, alien sea monster, or plumbing worthy of a Ridley Scott set.

Breathing equipment was necessary to go into the deeper sections, or the ominous 'moon well' that sank right through the structure to the bottom. Distant noises of the sea and wind were replaced by muffled waves and the clanks of submarine steel as you descended below sea level.[84]

The occupation garnered little attention at first from the British press. However, the occupiers kept sending news releases and giving interviews. The campaign had great visual appeal, and Greenpeace got extensive news coverage in other parts of Europe thanks to the organization's well-developed communications capacity.

During the occupation, Greenpeace insisted that the Brent Spar should be brought to shore and recycled instead of being dumped. In addition to preventing pollution, recycling the Spar's steel and other materials would save about 200 terajoules of energy, "roughly equivalent to the annual energy consumption of 1,300 people."[85]

Greenpeace activists in front of the Brent Spar, deluged
by firefighting water streams from Shell vessels.
(Greenpeace / David Sims)

THE BOYCOTT

As the occupation of the Spar was underway, environmental and social justice organizations launched a boycott campaign against Shell in Germany. They were concerned not only about ocean dumping but also about Shell's treatment of the Indigenous Ogoni people in Nigeria.

Anti-Shell campaigns in Germany grew quickly. At the time, Shell had about 1,700 gas stations in Germany. Protests happened at hundreds of them, including property destruction and at least one instance of arson. Even children put up homemade posters on Shell stations calling for a boycott.[86]

The boycott was supported not only on the German left but across the political spectrum. The pro-business Liberal Free Democratic party and even the *German police* announced that they would not use Shell gasoline.[87]

The boycott spread to other parts of Europe and was joined by politicians, including the Danish prime minister, the Dutch economics minister, and the Swedish environment minister.[88]

Newspapers encouraged readers to join the boycott, with the UK *Observer* proclaiming: "Shell will only see sense if hit in the pocket."[89]

Shell's PR response was lackluster, partly because Shell bosses were so convinced they were right. One misogynistic Shell executive told a management seminar: "Arguing with Greenpeace is like arguing with your wife: what have facts got to do with it?"[90]

Here's a fact: by the summer of 1995, the boycott was costing Shell millions of dollars a day.[91]

THE STRIKE FORCE

As the boycott grew, the UK Government became fed up with the campaigns and the Brent Spar occupation. By June 1995, government officials secretly ordered a thirty-two-person team of marines to prepare to storm and take over the Spar by Wednesday, June 21.[92] Marines who were trained to deal with maritime hijacking gathered intelligence and carried out simulations of an attack on the Spar. They planned to rappel down to the platform from helicopters.[93]

Rose explains:

> Earlier events had probably predisposed the Major Government to take a punitive line against Greenpeace. In a campaign against nuclear proliferation, Greenpeace had embarrassed the Navy by successfully delaying the sea passage of a Trident nuclear submarine leaving its Scottish base in 1994. At Easter 1995, it had mounted a peaceable "invasion" of the nuclear reprocessing plant at Sellafield. Again, this was in protest at proliferation and the plant's role in producing plutonium which is shipped to the bomb-making facility at Aldermaston.
>
> At Aldermaston itself, Greenpeace blocked a pipe discharging radioactive waste into the Thames. Both events received considerable, and global, television coverage, timed as they were on the eve of nuclear Non-Proliferation Treaty talks in New York.
>
> As a result of the Aldermaston action, MoD Police raided the UK office of Greenpeace in May during the 'Spar campaign, seizing documents, "hoovering" computers, and subsequently visiting campaigners' homes and taking them to police stations for questioning over possible charges of criminal conspiracy.[94]

Also that June, Shell quietly organized its own helicopter strike force comprising Shell security officers and police. They planned to storm the Spar and arrest the occupiers—and then sink the Spar where it was to finish the issue once and for all.[95]

On June 20, Shell's helicopters were on their way to the North Sea when they paused at Stornoway Airport to refuel. But before they could take off, they got a sudden order from Shell management to wait. Helicopters full of security officers and police sat on the runway, rotors spinning.

At the last possible moment, the CEO of Shell made a surprise announcement: Shell would capitulate. Shell agreed not to sink the Spar. Instead, it would be salvaged, with the superstructure either reused or recycled. The helicopter strike force returned home.

British government officials were angry and caught off guard by Shell's abrupt surrender. But the pressure on Shell had become overwhelming. Sales in Germany alone had dropped 50 percent—Shell literally could not afford to keep ignoring the public outcry.[96]

The victory was substantial. Greenpeace organizers and their allies did more than just prevent a massive corporation from dumping the Brent Spar and the ocean contamination it would have caused. They set a new precedent against ocean dumping. For decades, their victory prevented government and industry from using the ocean to dump other obsolete infrastructure—including about 100 other offshore oil and gas rigs.[97]

Sometime later, Shell announced that the Brent Spar would be towed to shore for salvage and that the main superstructure would be reused as a dockside building.[98]

WHY THEY WON

The Brent Spar victory was a classic example of full spectrum resistance. The *diversity of tactics* used was critical to success. The campaign spanned a continuum of action, from massive boycotts to awareness-raising to government advocacy to direct action.

These diverse tactics did not conflict with each other—they were perfectly complementary and strengthened each other.

If Greenpeace had not used direct action to occupy the Brent Spar, boycotts in Germany would never have begun. The power of mass boycotts in Europe *protected* the activists by using *economic force* to ensure that Shell would capitulate. (Boycott organizers also understood that Shell was more vulnerable to economic force than the UK government.) Without that complementary economic disruption, a helicopter strike team would have put a violent end to the Brent Spar takeover in June 1995.

What's more, groups and movements using different tactics were able to cooperate and build solidarity. The church and environmental groups organizing the German boycotts did not condemn direct action on the Brent Spar—they avoided falling into the trap of becoming the "good protesters" in contrast to the militants. They celebrated direct action; indeed, some of the German protest groups were very militant and damaged Shell gas stations, a move that made even Greenpeace a bit uncomfortable.

Likewise, the people advocating for international agreements to protect oceans (like the OSPAR Convention) did not attack Greenpeace for "working outside the system," nor did the Spar occupiers condemn international agreements as "reformist." People understood that *they were all working together* toward the common objective of protecting the ocean.

This deep solidarity meant that each person and group could use the tactics best matched to their skills and capacities, whether mobilizing their church congregation to boycott Shell or captaining a ship to seize an abandoned oil platform.

The campaign was surprisingly quick—only fifty-one days passed from the April 30 occupation of the Spar to Shell's capitulation on June 20, 1995. Despite this, campaign organizers also developed international *solidarity* with other movements, particularly with Ogoni resistance in Nigeria, where leaders like Ken Saro-Wiwa struggled to assert Indigenous autonomy against Shell and the Nigerian military government.[99]

Occupation can be a risky movement tactic for two reasons: logistical depletion and violent repression. In the case of *logistical depletion*, a movement's resources and morale are drained by the need to supply a prolonged —and eventually tiresome— action. During instances of *violent repression*, people are physically attacked. The Occupy Movement suffered from both of these problems.

For these reasons, resistance occupations are often brief. Civil rights sit-ins in the 1960s usually lasted only a few hours. The Brent Spar campaign succeeded quickly, but the occupation was *not* brief—fifty-one days of isolation on an abandoned oil spar is very difficult, and Greenpeace's well-developed logistical capacity was critical to the movement's success. Organizers could rely on years of expertise, infrastructure like ships and boats, and donations from a broad network of supporters. A handful of highly committed volunteers also sustained the occupation and didn't have to worry about maintaining the morale of hundreds of untrained or inexperienced participants who might simply get bored.

However, activists involved in the Brent Spar action were always at risk of violent repression. Many occupations have been dispersed that way, from the 1916 Easter Rising in Ireland to the 2018 anti-pipeline blockaders at Standing Rock. Greenpeace narrowly avoided this outcome at the Brent Spar through diverse tactics, especially *deterrence*.

The British government had the military force required to crush the tiny, unarmed occupation and was ready to do so. But the consequences for Shell would have been worse. The boycott would have grown and spread, and any violent repression would have quickly been pushed out to screens and newspapers around the world.

The struggle over the Brent Spar is part of a tradition of powerful resistance against fossil fuel companies and extractive imperialism, a struggle that has continued at Standing Rock and Unist'ot'en, and against nuclear waste dumps in South Australia.

It's easy to be awed by the boldness and technical capabilities that allowed Greenpeace to succeed. However, most of the political force created in the campaign was generated by small, community-level groups that organized boycotts and direct action against Shell.

We have the capabilities to generate that political and economic leverage as long as we are willing to use a mix of disruptive tactics for both direct and indirect action.

It is well past time for that to happen on a large scale. By the 1980s, Shell was already raising North Sea oil platforms to anticipate rising sea levels. Shell and other oil companies have had a detailed understanding of climate change since the 1960s but buried their research and funded public disinformation campaigns so that they could keep profiteering at the expense of people and the planet.

We can't go back in time to change what fossil fuel companies did in the 1960s, 1970s, or 1980s. However, we *can* be part of a tradition of movements that fight effectively against those corporations today.

It's too late to undo corporate lies about global warming, but it's not too late to change and escalate our tactics and learn from powerful examples like the victory at the Brent Spar.

FIVE

Spies for Peace and the Committee of 100

UNITED KINGDOM
1963

In 1963, a group of British anti-war activists called the Spies for Peace broke into a secret government bunker and exposed state plans for nuclear war. Their revelations shocked the country and galvanized the anti-war movement.

THE CAMPAIGN FOR NUCLEAR DISARMAMENT

The modern peace movement was—symbolically, at least—birthed in Britain in 1958. With the horrors of World War II still fresh in national consciousness, there was growing public concern about the potential that the wars of the future would be *nuclear* wars that could extinguish human life on Earth.

During preparations for an ad hoc demonstration against nuclear arms in the UK, organizer Gerald Holtom designed a new symbol using the semaphore for the letters "N D," for "nuclear disarmament." This symbol would spread across the world as part of a growing peace movement. Some people today still associate it with peace, love, and groovy hippies.

But for early organizers, the connotations were apocalyptic.

As organizer Peggy Duff explained, they made badges using the symbol out of ceramic rather than plastic because "if nuclear war came and we all went up in nuclear fire, the badges would survive and remain as our memorial, to be found maybe centuries later by whatever [people] managed to survive the holocaust."[100]

That was the feeling in the air in 1958 when scattered anti-nuclear organizers in the Britain coalesced into the biggest movement of its time: the Campaign for Nuclear Disarmament, or CND.

CND was a "big tent" organization with people from many diverse backgrounds. It included committed direct-action organizers—like Pat Arrowsmith and Michael Randle—who initiated and coordinated an anti-nuclear march that became an annual tradition. There were churchgoers and atheists, artists and professors, wealthy elites, labor activists, communists, and anarchists.

PEGGY DUFF, first general secretary of CND. Noam Chomsky called her "one of the people who really changed modern history."

CANON JOHN COLLINS, chair of CND. Unfortunately, Duff recalled, he was paternalistic and "basically lacked the imagination or the courage to accept and lead the movement as it was."[101]

That diversity came in part from the sheer number of participants. At its height, CND mobilized over 100,000 people. At its first major speaking event (in London, February 1958), CND had to rent five halls for overflow seating and transmit the speakers' voices by radio. The mood was one of powerful excitement—the audience decided to stage an impromptu march to Downing Street right afterward, where multiple people were arrested.[102]

Many CND organizers believed strongly in Non-Violent Direct Action (NVDA) and civil disobedience. Indeed, if CND had committed itself to direct action, backed by 100,000 people, it would very likely have succeeded in its goal of causing Britain to renounce nuclear weapons unilaterally.

However, CND's potential was curtailed by a group of very powerful people—its executive committee. The initially self-ap-

PAT ARROWSMITH was co-founder of CND, part of the Direct Action Committee and C100. She was also a Fulbright Scholar, a lesbian, and a prolific author who served 11 prison sentences for her direct action.

MICHAEL RANDLE organized with CND's Direct Action Committee and C100, and was a long-time peace activist who spent time in prison for his actions.

pointed executive committee desperately worked to suppress the more radical energies of its membership to maintain the sympathies of people in the government.

Consider the words of Peggy Duff, an organizer who became the general secretary of the CND. According to Duff, executive committee members "were basically very British, conservative, and rather naïve. They thought that banning the bomb was a fairly simple matter and they never recognized the revolution in British politics that it required."[103]

If the executive committee had been made up of *moderates* who preferred conversation to conflict, that would have been one thing. But they were also *liberals* who, as Duff explained, wanted profound change without having to upset daily life or the prevailing structures of power.

They were liberals in large part because of their privilege and class positions, which they sought to maintain. The president of CND, Lord Bertrand Russell, was a famed anti-imperialist, peace activist, and Nobel laureate, but he supported the aristocracy. Liberals stand apart from progressive radicals who place the success of struggle above personal status and gain. Pat Arrowsmith, for example, worked as a nursing assistant but was fired after she invited patients and staff to sign an anti-nuclear petition.

Chief among the liberals was Canon John Collins, a priest in the Church of England who would serve for many years as the chair of CND and its executive committee. By church standards, Canon Collins was boldly political. But he was also a rule follower and rule enforcer (perhaps not surprising since his title of "Canon" literally means "church law"). As a member of the upper ranks of the Church hierarchy, Collins was used to giving instructions and having them followed—which was a cause of the trouble to come.

After CND's founding in 1958, the anti-nuclear movement grew and became more militant. An arms-length direct action committee had already formed (including Pat Arrowsmith as secretary and Michael Randle as chair), which organized a march from London to Aldermaston, the site of the government's Atomic Weapons Establishment. (This march became an annual tradition.)

At first, CND's executive committee supported this event, which was a low-risk form of action. CND general secretary Peggy Duff recounted: "The march was tremendously successful and gave the movement a great lift."[104] However, she added, the executive committee worried that they did not have enough control over the march and began to develop an "anxiety about rival organizations which later became almost an obsession with some of the leaders of CND."[105]

The executive committee tried to rein in potential direct action and asked to integrate march organizing more firmly into its hierarchy, a proposition that was declined by march organizers, Pat Arrowsmith in particular.

This internal conflict worsened in late 1958. The increasingly popular direct action committee organized a series of nonviolent demonstrations against the construction of new "Thor" missile bases. These first ballistic missiles were built in the United States and tipped with thermonuclear warheads.*

CND direct actionists traveled to a Thor missile base that was being built in Norfolk. Peggy Duff described the missile bases as looking "very sinister" with "three long black sheds in which the three missiles were housed, surrounded by a galaxy of gantries and miles of barbed wire. They were usually situated on a high, bare plateau."[106]

Duff wrote: "It was dusk when the Direct Action group reached the missile base at North Pickenham and as they attempted to enter it the sun was setting, red and fiery, behind the base. The operation was nonviolent only on one side."[107]

---

* These were *intermediate-range* rather than *intercontinental* ballistic missiles, and so their reach was limited. However, weapons positioned in the UK could strike Moscow.

The nonviolent demonstrators were attacked by construction laborers, who stuffed at least one anti-nuclear demonstrator into a cement mixer. Press reports on the event were muddled, failing to differentiate between CND in general and the arm's length Direct Action Committee in particular—one report even used the term "sabotage" even though no sabotage occurred. Duff writes: "I don't know who was most annoyed—the direct action committee which lost the credit for the operation, or the campaign whose leaders didn't want it."[108]

Canon Collins issued a statement distancing CND from "sabotage" and "violence."[109] As Duff explained: "There were three difficulties about this statement. First, it implied that sabotage had been intended. Second, it also implied that the action had provoked violence or was responsible for violence occurring. Third, it was unquestionably a dissociation and, as such, infuriated both the direct action committee and thousands of campaigners who were delighted with the project and the publicity it got."[110]

Because direct action was so popular among rank-and-file campaigners, after Collins's statement, "the campaign exploded in wrath, and the next meeting of the executive committee was forced to issue a statement that, in future, it should not, as far as possible, publicly repudiate nor formally associate itself with actions involving civil disobedience."

But among the grassroots, demand for direct action remained high. Grassroots CND participants had a strong sense of the campaign's momentum and potential power if they decided to escalate. Grassroots members also identified more with the ethics driving their actions than their social status. At CND's first annual conference (in March 1959), Pat Arrowsmith put forward a resolution that CND, in general, should commit to civil disobedience. Duff recounts: "It seemed very likely that [the resolution] would be accepted by a considerable majority. The executive committee, in a panic, made it clear that if this happened, they would resign in a body."[111] Because of this threat, the resolution was defeated.

There were some further attempts to harmonize civil disobedience within CND.[112] But it became clear to many of CND's most active members that, with an executive committee that continued to hold them back, they required a new organization—one that was not so timid and compliant with authority, and one that would briefly become the most powerful and effective movement in Britain.

THE COMMITTEE OF 100

While many in CND's grassroots were chaffing under the restrictions of the executive committee, discontent had spread even to the upper ranks. CND President Lord Bertrand Russell was a renowned logician, and despite his social status, he could see for himself that more direct tactics were needed. For some time, Russell had wished to speak publicly in favor of direct action, but CND Chair Canon Collins had insisted against it.

In 1961, Russell resigned as president of CND, arguing that the organization was suppressing civil disobedience. He joined a new organization, Committee of 100, which formed to correct CND's limitations and deficiencies. Inspired by other movements around the world—including the American civil rights movement—the Committee of 100 sought to bring mass nonviolent direct action to the UK.

Committee members approached organizing with an attitude of radical transparency. In the beginning, 100 people signed a document claiming joint responsibility for their actions—hence their name, the Committee of 100. The new organization included Bertrand Russell (soon elected as president), Pat Arrowsmith, Michael Randle (as secretary), and other key activists from CND and the direct action committee, as well as celebrities like actor Vanessa Redgrave.

To avoid the problems with the CND, the Committee of 100 (C100) used a largely anarchist and increasingly decentralized approach to planning. In this way, C100 initiated a series of mass direct actions against militarism and nuclear arms, hoping to get the British government to stop participating in nuclear escalation.

In February 1961, they held "the first-ever large-scale public sit-down demonstration in Britain" outside the War Ministry, impressively mobilizing 5,000 participants.[113] Their declaration called for an end to the nuclear arms race: "We call upon people from all walks of life to take direct action to bring the production of nuclear weapons to a halt. Our action today is the first step in a campaign of nonviolent civil disobedience. We hereby serve notice on our Government that we can no longer stand aside while they prepare to destroy mankind."[114]

Peggy Duff spoke with warmth about that day: "There was a feeling about the square that day which I found later in Paris during May and June 1968—a feeling of revolution, of real challenge."[115]

The government and police response to this first event was quite tolerant, much to the organizers' disappointment, who understood that their victory would require provocation and disruption. Bertrand Russell said: "Our movement depends for its success on an immense public opinion, and we cannot create that unless we rouse the authorities to more action than they took yesterday."[116] From that perspective, it was fortunate that their second major demonstration led to 826 arrests out of a crowd of 2,500.[117]

Their third demonstration, planned for September 1961, finally got the response some organizers desired—the government invoked the Public Order Act of 1936 to try to block the protest and summoned thirty-six of the C100 signatories to court to compel them to agree to a peace bond. (Some thirty-two of them refused the summons.)

This government repression was great news for C100's profile and popularity. Nuclear war was horrifying, to be sure, but it also felt distant and abstract. However, a government ban on a public protest felt *personal*, a breach of civil liberties that was more than a little reminiscent of the fascist or totalitarian governments that were supposed to be the enemies of the UK.

Hence, the attempted protest ban boosted public support for the Committee of 100 to truly impressive levels. C100 went ahead with a September 1961 demonstration in Trafalgar Square, mobilizing an incredible 12,000 people for their sit-in.

Over 1,300 people were arrested, which was very much in line with the Committee of 100's core strategy: *fill the jails*.[118] Committee organizers believed that if they could mobilize increasing numbers of people—thousands or tens of thousands over many actions—the government would have no choice but to back down and end the nuclear arms race. After a series of successful actions in London, the C100 planned to expand their nonviolent action to include military bases, including RAF Wethersfield military airbase.

The government responded with more repression. The military built new twelve-foot fences around several bases and warned that sentries could shoot protesters who entered the bases.

While the members of the Committee of 100 could claim equal responsibility, that claim didn't compel the government to treat them equally. So, in December 1961, the government arrested six well-known C100 organizers and laid conspiracy charges against them. After a controversial trial, the five men arrested were given eighteen-month prison sentences—Michael Randle among them.

The single woman charged, Helen Allegranza, received a twelve-month sentence, much to her disgust. She stood up and demanded the court give her fair treatment—the longer sentence that her male counterparts received—but the court refused.

As the government intended, this conspiracy trial had a chilling effect on the movement overall. Over 7,000 people still went to

Wethersfield to protest—not as many as the 50,000 that C100 had originally aspired to mobilize, but nonetheless impressive.

While some people were intimidated, others became more radical. Prison sentences are meant to intimidate, but they can also deepen a political prisoner's commitment.

Which brings us to the Spies for Peace.

THE BUNKER HEIST

The Spies for Peace were a group of eight people, including key participants from the Committee of 100, who decided to creatively escalate their tactics.

There is a common narrative that militants are isolated malcontents on the "fringe" of social movements. However, the opposite is more often true. In fact—in the case of Nelson Mandela and many others—militants and radicals are often among the most experienced, thoughtful, and well-connected people in their movements.

This was very much the case in the Spies for Peace. We know this because several Spies for Peace "came out" later in life and discussed their experiences. Two of them had served eighteen-month sentences because of their work organizing mass nonviolent action with the C100. Three had been signatories of a pamphlet titled *Beyond Counting Arses*, which encouraged the C100 to think about more than just the *number* of participants and consider how they could adapt their tactics so that each participating person had a greater impact.

Far from fringe malcontents, the Spies for Peace were dedicated, thoughtful, self-sacrificing, and well-connected—all qualities that would help their group achieve success.

In February 1963, four members of the Spies for Peace followed a tip-off that there was a secret government bunker near the town of Reading. After exploring cold and muddy fields, the Spies for Peace were able to locate a fenced-off hill with a few unmarked structures just west of the village of Warren Row. While the site was on a farm, a suspiciously large number of radio aerials were nearby, with cables leading into the hill.

They were able to gain entry to one of the buildings, a brick boiler house, through an exterior door.* Once inside, they found a steep staircase leading down into the interior of the hill. At the bottom of the stairs, the four activists found an office complex full of desks and government documents. It looked like the office was in active use— as if someone had just stepped out for tea—so they photographed documents, collected information, and then quickly and quietly left.

It was clear to them that the bunker was an administrative center-in-waiting to be used by regional government in case of a nuclear war. Shortly after, the Spies for Peace sent a different group of four, better prepared to collect information, back to the bunker. They spotted workers on the site, so the Spies for Peace waited at a nearby pub until the workers left and then picked the lock of the exterior door. As Natasha Walter (daughter of a participant) explains: "This time, they spent several hours there. One took photographs. One copied documents. One traced maps. One went through every drawer and every cabinet. Then they left with a suitcase full of copied papers and a camera full of photographs."[119]

Off-site, with a full group of eight people, the Spies for Peace compiled the documents into a pamphlet titled *Danger! Official Secret: RSG-6*. Working in a barn, they printed 4,000 copies of their booklet and anonymously mailed thousands of copies. They then meticulously disposed of all evidence that could connect them to the pamphlets.

---

* There is conflicting information about how the building was accessed the first time. Natasha Walter says the building was unlocked; Sam Carroll says that the front door was "easy to break into." For the second visit, however, both sources agree that the boiler room door was locked and had to be picked.

VICTORIES AND LEGACY

At first, the government tried to keep journalists from reporting on the leaked documents. However, after a radio station in Czechoslovakia read all the documents on the air, the British government gave up.

Regular people in Britain were shocked by what the documents revealed. The 1950s had been the era of "duck and cover" when governments portrayed nuclear attacks as something that one could survive by hiding under a desk.

Instead, the documents made it clear that the government had absolutely no hope of protecting the general population from the horrifying consequences of nuclear war. Furthermore, the government had built a series of underground bunkers—the Regional Seats of Government—which would host the unelected administrators of a post-apocalyptic state in waiting.

The effect was a permanent shift in popular attitudes toward nuclear war. It became clearer to everyday people that—rather than protecting them from foreign enemies—the nuclear arms race was a threat to regular people in every country and that government elites didn't have their wellbeing at heart.

This shift in attitudes was a vindication of the anarchist approaches of organizers. It also gave a substantial boost to the anti-war movement (much to the horror of CND's Canon Collins, who, against Peggy Duff's advice, virulently condemned the Spies for Peace in a television interview).[120]

The next major anti-nuclear march was diverted, against the wishes of CND organizers, to pass by the secret bunker at Regional Seat of Government-6. The leaked documents galvanized many people. The Spies for Peace accomplished what they had set out to do without any arrests or jail time.

The new information, however, was not enough to reverse

declining participation in mass civil disobedience organized by the Committee of 100. For the reasons mentioned below, the group could not mobilize enough people to completely "fill the jails."

In 1963, the anti-nuclear movement also had some success on the international scale with the signing of Partial Nuclear Test Ban Treaty in August 1963. The Treaty banned testing of nuclear weapons in the atmosphere, outer space, and underwater, and was signed by the USSR, the UK, and the USA.

Pressure from widespread protests helped to make this agreement happen.[121] As President Dwight Eisenhower once remarked while in London, "I like to believe that people, in the long run, are going to do more to promote peace than our governments. Indeed, I think that people want peace so much that one of these days governments had better get out of the way and let them have it."[122]

Some of the people involved with C100 believed, as Dr. Sam Carroll writes, "that during the Cuba Crisis the peace movement may have given the world leaders an excuse to climb down without losing face. Whilst not entirely committed to this perspective, Michael Randle is keen to keep the idea alive and laughs as he says: 'maybe we saved the world from being blown up.'"[123][124]

While important, the Partial Nuclear Test Ban Treaty of 1963 may have accelerated the decline of anti-nuclear organizing by making some participants feel that governments were now capable of handling the problem. At the same time, resisters had other developing crises to respond to in the 1960s. The Committee of 100 dissolved in 1968 as key organizers moved on to new campaigns dealing with issues like homelessness and the Vietnam War.[125]

However, the Committee of 100 still had a profound and lasting effect on organizing in the UK. A critical part of their goal was to popularize mass nonviolent direct action tactics in the UK, and they did it. They also trained a generation of people in decentralized organizing tactics. While they weren't able to end the Cold

War, they put enormous pressure on government, and may even have given governments an excuse to back down in emergencies like the 1962 Cuban Missile Crisis.

In the 2010s, several participants in Spies for Peace finally revealed themselves, giving us the crucial behind-the-scenes details needed to understand how they pulled off their heist. When asked why they spoke up after so many years, participant Mike Lesser explained that they wished "to show what was possible with a little ingenuity. There was also an element of criticism of the present level of resistance."

COMPARING CAPACITIES

The CND, C100, and Spies for Peace were organized in fundamentally different ways. In some cases, their movement capacities were in harmony with their overall goals; in other ways, there was dysfunction. Let's compare.

Recruitment and Training: CND and the Committee of 100 relied on open calls for action and extensive mass media coverage. C100 also held training workshops in nonviolence for participants, and their increasingly decentralized organizing style emphasized participation and helped to train a new generation of activists.

The Spies for Peace were "invitation only" and drew from a pool of more experienced and committed activists.

Groups and Organization: CND was relatively centralized and very structured—which didn't necessarily correspond with its effectiveness. Peggy Duff writes that "CND spawned an incredible number of committees, groups, regional councils, specialist sections, *ad hoc* committees, planning groups. The number was not always directly related to its vitality. They tended to increase as its impact lessened."[126]

"The first and foremost was the self-appointed Executive Committee of 1958 with all its big names," she adds. But she also notes that the executive committee was "clearly unrepresentative" of the grassroots.[127]

The pamphlet *Beyond Counting Arses* was much more critical, calling CND leadership bureaucratic and largely self-perpetuating, arguing that it became unmoored from its supporters, and until the leaders were "betraying the very principles on which its movement was based."[128] Their assessment of CND in early 1963 was quite blunt: "CND has degenerated as an organization beyond the point where it is worth trying to reform it."[129]

The Committee of 100 was organized in part as a reaction to this. While the C100 was originally more London-oriented and more "elite-run" according to Sam Carroll, its organizing style shifted over time. As it became more decentralized, with regional working groups, grassroots activists had increasing influence on the tone and direction of the C100's work and tactics.

Because C100 was so large, they created a series of specialized groups and roles including "welfare, international, publicity, schools, treasury, speakers, present action, future action, trade unions, and the working group (i.e. management or executive committee). At least one person from each group was to be on the working group."[130]

However, this eventually became a problem. It is difficult for an organization of thousands of people to organize by consensus, especially when that organization is open to new participants without a unifying political approach and especially when it is engaged in a dangerous struggle in which people risk arrest and violence.

The signatories of *Beyond Counting Arses* argued that, by 1963, the C100 had "taken its libertarian methods of organisation to absurd extremes." Furthermore, the pamphlet argued, "The way in which a determined minority can prevent any decisions being reached has paralyzed the London and National Committees for some months. The result has usually been compromises that have pleased few and satisfied none. The Committee's continual production of innocuous leaflets is a case in point."[131]

Agreement was required from many different groups within C100: "The very process of decision-making has become ridiculously diffuse: one proposal may be flung back and forth between the National Committee, its Planning and Working Groups, regional committees, area working groups, and so on."[132] At any point, in any of these groups, people could block the process, so that by 1963 most important actions "took place in spite of rather than through the Committee's normal structure."[133]

While C100's approach was anarchistic in many ways, there were still some problematic tendencies from CND. In particular, *Beyond Counting Arses* argues: "The do-it-yourself philosophy on which the Committee has developed is in flat contradiction to its reliance on Big Names. The Committee of 100 has become mesmerised by Bertrand Russell as its spokesman."[134] Lord Russell canceled a planned mass action by the committee "in the face of enormous opposition from its own militants."[135]

Eventually, Russell and other celebrities began to leave the organization. "The way in which the Committee has been damaged by the resignations of Vanessa Redgrave and Bertrand Russell is a measure of the extent to which we have used the publicity value of Big Names rather than carefully formulating our own collective ideas."[136]

The organizational approach of the Spies for Peace was a response to C100's shortcomings and representative of the classic differences between aboveground and underground groups.

The C100 began as a public list of its endorsers, but membership in the Spies for Peace was strictly secret. The Spies for Peace began with five people and then increased to eight. Historically speaking, this range seems to be the sweet spot for an underground cell. Spies for Peace also had specialized roles internally.

While the Spies for Peace are not widely known, they have been remembered by anarchists in particular. Until recently, the lack of information has created some misunderstandings about how the group organized. One anarchist publication notes how the Spies for Peace developed their "top secret" booklet, emphasizing the ad hoc nature of their approach:

"Messages were passed from mouth to mouth along the route, documents from hand to hand. One group passed a secret to a second, which then set about reprinting it. A caravan became the source of a leaflet, a shopping basket a distribution centre. A hundred copies of a pamphlet are distributed in the streets: some are sure to reach the people who will distribute them."[137]

While this sounds nice, the reality was often the opposite. Distribution was far from ad hoc; the core group produced thousands of copies and mailed them to specific supporters who might reproduce them. Nonhierarchical, underground groups have to do *more* planning, not less. They have to be more precise and think things through further in advance.

Consider the security practices of the Spies for Peace.

Security and Safety: The Spies for Peace were very security-conscious, especially when it came to operational security. Their booklet was partially typewritten, but every typewriter is unique, and the letters produce a slightly different impression on the page compared with other typewriters. A microscopic inspection of typewritten text could lead back, forensically, to a specific typewriter.* As a result, immediately after the group finished typing the document, they threw the typewriter into a river.

To ensure that they did not leave any fingerprints, members

---

* Some modern printers have tracking technology built in. For example, it was revealed in the 2000s that some color printers secretly added a nearly-invisible pattern of yellow dots to print-outs, which could be traced back to that printer.

wore gloves while picking locks, assembling leaked documents, and handling envelopes used to mail out thousands of copies.

Members had specific roles, never took notes at meetings, and received information on a "need-to-know" basis. For example, the person responsible for getting stamps and envelopes would not reveal where they had purchased them or whether anyone might have donated money to purchase the supplies.

Mailings were made from several locations around London. Members even mailed copies to themselves and thousands of others to ensure they did not stand out in any way.

Despite their best efforts, there were some potential issues. Specifically, they lacked a firewall separating aboveground and underground. Many of those involved in Spies for Peace were active members of the Committee of 100, had spent time in prison for their aboveground direct actions, and were well-known to the police. Indeed, some of their homes were raided after the leak as police desperately tried to find the Spies.

However, the Spies' careful security measures prevented the police from obtaining any evidence linking known protesters to the action.

The absence of a firewall could have been a problem, except for two important factors.

First, the action was a "one-off." By the time the police raids began, the Spies for Peace had already destroyed any evidence that could have been used against them. If members had been committing an ongoing series of clandestine illegal actions, it might have been difficult for them to stay safe.

Second, the police tracking technology of 1963 was primitive compared to the surveillance technology of today. Whistleblowers today require a much higher level of technical ability and tradecraft than they did in 1963.* Simultaneously operating in

---

* Many whistleblowers or data leakers of today—like Reality Winner, Edward Snowden, and Chelsea Manning—were exposed, unable to keep their identities secret.

underground and aboveground groups without a firewall would be a much greater risk now.

It's also worth noting that some members of Spies for Peace—especially young ones—were anxious about being exposed for years afterward. Fortunately, that did not happen.

The other two organizations in this story were less security-oriented. CND and C100 relied on safety in numbers.

Communication: In general, CND and C100 had an impressive communications capacity. The 3,000-piece mailing could not have happened without the communications connections Spies for Peace cultivated through the Committee of 100.

Intel and Recon: Spies for Peace and the Committee of 100 relied on reconnaissance and intelligence gathering. Once the C100 decided to move beyond demonstrations in London to actions at military bases, they had to organize scouting missions so that they could plan effectively.[138]

Spies for Peace relied entirely on intelligence and reconnaissance capacities.

Counterintel and Repression: Many forms of repression were used against these organizations:

1. Surveillance was undoubtedly used by the government. But the C100 was so open that, at least in the beginning, surveillance was barely necessary. The Spies for Peace were careful enough that surveillance would have been ineffective.

2. Psychological Warfare and Propaganda were used against C100, especially once the organization decided to escalate to actions at military bases. The government warned that they would use everything from legal prosecution to lethal force against protestors.

3. Infiltration and Informers were likely used against C100, but it's unclear to what extent. We can assume that government infiltrators and informers were active in the C100, but not much has been written about this. Since actions were planned so publicly, infiltrators wouldn't have gathered a lot of useful tactical intelligence. (The Spies for Peace would have been protected against this by their tight security practices.)

4. The Legal System: C100 participants were targeted for legal repression and jail sentences, especially through conspiracy cases.

5. Illegal Violence: The government threatened to shoot those who trespassed onto military bases, and police roughed up people they arrested. But this type of violence was nothing like the scale of that used to repress other movements (e.g., Irish Independence movements).

6. Martial Law and Population Control: Under the Official Secrets Act, the government would have escalated further had the number of C100 participants continued to grow.

7. Selective Concessions and Co-optation may have been at work. To some extent, the CND leadership was neutralized by the false belief that they would win concessions through persuasion. That was not a government tactic so much as a character flaw of the self-appointed leadership. Selective concessions were rarely used in a targeted way against the C100. However, the Partial Nuclear Test Ban Treaty in 1963 caused some decline in campaign participation.

Because of their careful security practices, Spies for Peace were largely immune to most of these forms of repression.

Logistics and Fundraising: Logistics was a big challenge for Spies for Peace because they had to secretly acquire supplies (paper, envelopes, stamps) and dispose of anything that could link individual members to the action.

One member of the Spies for Peace traveled across London to buy paper from multiple stores and purchased a quantity that would seem unremarkable from each store. However, another activist, interviewed by Sam Carroll, recalled buying a huge amount of paper and taking it in a taxi straight to Spies for Peace member Nicolas Walter's house. In retrospect, this would have been a substantial risk and highlights the importance of a firewall between aboveground and underground activities.

There were many other people in supportive roles who were active in C100 but not members of Spies for Peace. In a more proper example of a firewall, several of them received anonymous copies of the *Danger! Official Secret: RSG-6* pamphlet; they were able to mass-produce additional copies to redistribute them.

For the Committee of 100, however, logistics eventually became a limiting factor. They relied on *mass* civil disobedience, mobilizing thousands of people for nonviolent direct action. When their actions were focused on London, they could rely on people finding their own transportation. However, later in their campaigns, the committee expanded their scope to plan mass actions at military bases across the UK.

Transportation became a huge barrier to these actions, so logistics became a weak point that the government could use against the resisters. For example, after the committee had chartered buses from a private company to bring protesters to RAF Wethersfield, the government revoked the bus company's operating licenses.[139]

Actions and Tactics: The debate over tactics continued from the beginning of CND through C100. CND's refusal to use civil disobedience was its chief weakness.

"The Campaign has done a useful job of developing a mass awareness of the danger of nuclear war," explain the signatories of

Beyond Counting Arses. "But its whole emphasis on 'pressurising' [sic] politicians . . . is based on a profound illusion and condemns the movement to an impotence now perceived by thousands."[140]

"We live in an increasingly authoritarian society, in which the powers that be are quite capable of coping with opposition directed through the traditional channels. These traditional channels of protest have themselves become built-in stabilisers of the whole society."[141]

The Committee of 100 had two key tactical understandings from the beginning. First, they understood that disruptive direct action was necessary. Second, they understood that such action had to *escalate* over time.

However, their approach also had tactical shortcomings, particularly the challenges of perpetual escalation. When C100 announced their action at Wethersfield, they claimed that 50,000 people would participate. When "only" 7,000 showed up, the action looked like a failure. If C100 had promised 1,000 people, then 7,000 would have looked like a huge success. Likewise, if they had kept their exact destination *secret* until the last day, perhaps they could have prevented government repression from being effective.

Beyond Counting Arses warned that by 1963, C100 mass tactics had become ineffective and that some of their marches had become so ritualistic that they no longer represented a threat to government policy. "Although the Committee of 100 has been extremely radical in its time, we now seem reduced to demonstrations consisting of a ritual pas-de-deux with the police . . . (All right son. You've made your point. Now walk along nicely into court.)"[142]

"Certainly, there is little to be achieved as a traditional small pressure group. But mass action does not have to mean a yearly orgasm in Whitehall or public conscience-washing in Trafalgar Square." *Beyond Counting Arses* begs for more creative tactics and new metrics:

"We have demanded mass action, and only seen this in terms of masses of people acting at one place and at one time. We have looked for new ideas, and yet imprisoned ourselves in the mass sit down. . . . At Wethersfield the state was so scared that it brought out the troops. At Greenham Common we queued up to be arrested. In the past our yardstick of success has usually been the total column inches in the Guardian or the number of arrested arses. We need new criteria on which to judge our actions."[143]

Beyond Counting Arses implores participants to move beyond the "fill the jails" approach and choose more decentralized, innovative, and disruptive tactics that maximize the impact that each participant can have. "We must attempt to hinder the warfare state in every possible way."[144] They suggest organizing within civil defense groups and coordinating strikes with unions. They identify various campaigns of disruption, including payphone-based mass calls to military and government phone systems and illegal publicity (like whitewashing hundreds of slogans across a town in one night).

They argue: "Most important of all, our actions must always be of the do-it-yourself type. We must understand that a victory won as a result of a struggle is valuable in itself. It heightens the self-confidence and self-reliance of those who have participated in it."

The Spies for Peace action was a perfect example of this because it took advantage of tactical principles like careful planning, surprise, and decentralized and simultaneous execution.

Campaigns and Strategy: With the goal of unilateral nuclear disarmament, CND had a *policy* but not an effective *strategy*. General Secretary Peggy Duff wrote: "They hoped that at some stage, sooner rather than later, so many marchers (or sitters) would gather in Whitehall that the Government would fall, and Lord Russell or Canon Collins, or both, would ride into the Kingdom on a white horse. What they would do then they rarely thought about. Occasional conferences on the positive aims of the campaign were very wishy washy."[145]

According to Peggy Duff, CND failed partly because of contradictions in its organizing style and because it drove out its own radicals. She explained: "Most campaigners wanted it both ways. They wanted to have their cake and eat it, to remain respectable within the establishment and to challenge it too, to operate inside and outside conventional politics . . . to remain inside the system and to destroy it."[146]

"Second," she adds, "the radical wing of the movement never succeeded in mounting a sharp enough challenge to swing the campaign abruptly from the old to the new. . . . And because so many sat and paid their fines and went home, the emphasis on personal action never overcame the ingrained habit of relying on leadership. *There were too many Canon Collins, not enough Michael Randles.*"[147]

Fundamentally, people like Canon Collins wanted to turn the nuclear disarmament movement from a diverse ecology of struggle into a monoculture of opinion and action. That approach undermined the impact of the movement as a whole.

It's easy to wonder what would have happened if the Committee of 100 had evolved differently to maximize impact with fewer people. Was it simply a victim of movement cycles as new tactical innovations were exhausted? Or could they have reinvigorated by following the advice of *Beyond Counting Arses*?

In any case, *Beyond Counting Arses* wasn't only about organization or tactics; it was about the grand strategy of social movements. The signatories of *Beyond Counting Arses* wanted the movement to think *militantly* and *radically*, to look for the shared roots of different struggles.

They argue: "The campaign against the Bomb must be linked to a great struggle for the protection and extension of our civil liberties."[148] Specifically, "we should publicly try to link up with locally organised struggles over conditions of work, increases in rent, etc. This is one case where a simple press statement, a leaflet or a public meeting could have a big impact. Although our ultimate aim should be a recognition of a common cause, we should realise that this is hardly an immediate prospect."[149]

This push was, perhaps, the most important legacy of the Committee of 100, as Sam Carroll describes:

> "The squatters' campaign, for example, was coordinated by C100 activists in their effort to combat homelessness in London. This type of community action inspired confidence in others to embark upon a new wave of Do-It-Yourself politics, resulting in a diversity of local protests throughout Britain. C100 also directly informed the ethos and NVDA [Non-Violent Direct Action] method of the women's movement and Greenham [Common] Peace Camp. By the 1980s even CND had adopted NVDA as protest policy and the much later environmental campaigns of today can also be traced back to C100. Another direction of influence rejected the notion of NVDA altogether and, maintaining the subversive spectacle approach, was spearheaded by the emergent Angry Brigade."[150]

The most experienced grassroots organizers involved in the struggle against the bomb came to understand the importance of movements that used diverse tactics, including solidarity across issues and organizations.

Beyond Counting Arses explores exactly that idea:

> We started off as a movement against "The Bomb." This struggle has led us to realise that our opponent is the state itself, and the social and economic interests it protects.

We discovered (some of us with surprise!) that our rulers, their government, their police, their courts and their press, act as a team to smash any real challenge to their bomb. We realised that the Labour Party and the Trades Union hierarchies are not alternatives to the established order. They are as much parts of the machinery of preservation as is Parliament itself.

We have had to learn, slowly and painfully and incompletely, that a solution to our problems can only come from ourselves. Neither parliament . . . [nor] the National Executive of CND can succeed on our behalf. . . .

The discovery that the Bomb is not an isolated cancer within an otherwise healthy society, but is in itself an example of society's basic rottenness, gives us common ground with those who are reaching similar conclusions about a society from their involvement of in other struggles.

"The shop stewards' movement and groups of militants in industry daily face misrepresentation by the mass media, the obstruction of their 'officials', the Special Branch and even court action in much the same way that we have. We have both heard the same kinds of screams from the establishment and the traditional left: 'Undemocratic! Subversive! Beatnik! Wildcat!' We are both drawing, tentatively, the same sorts of conclusions about society."

We cannot know which particular struggle will open the most eyes. We do know that each partial struggle is a part of the same fight.

It is the involvement of many people in many different issues that will finally raise the consciousness of the majority to the point where it can effectively challenge the state.

SIX

Wyhl Reactor Site Occupation

GERMANY

1975

Farmers took direct action in rural Germany to stop the construction of a nuclear reactor. Police repression almost quashed the movement, but the farmers prevailed, and the site became a nature reserve.

In 1969, Germany's first commercial nuclear power plant came online. At the time, electricity demand was rising rapidly in West Germany. The manufacturing industry had expanded rapidly in the "economic miracle" after World War II, and the West German government was eager to scale up electrical production to provide for the continued expansion of industry. In the early 1970s, the government decided to build eight new nuclear power plants across the country.

While the major nuclear accidents of the twentieth century had yet to happen—the Chernobyl meltdown did not occur until 1986—there was already some public concern about the safety of nuclear power plants and the disposal of nuclear waste.

As a result, the plan to build new reactors triggered pushback, particularly in the southwesternmost state of Baden-Württemberg. In 1972, environmentalists, farmers, and anti-nuclear activists staged protests and gathered 60,000 signatures to petition against a proposed reactor in Breisach. Their motto was "Better active today than radioactive tomorrow!"

The quick organizing worked. Because of the public outcry, the government decided to back off and cancel the plant in Breisach. However, the government began moving forward with another proposed reactor, which would have been the biggest in the world.[151] The government chose the community of Wyhl, an agricultural area known especially for grape-growing. It was a more rural and traditional area, and so—the government hoped—it would not be fertile ground for resistance.

In Wyhl, the government took a more proactive approach to propaganda, sending monthly mailings to residents to influence public opinion about nuclear power. Perhaps the government hoped that the outcry in Breisach was merely a "Not In My Back Yard" situation.

They were wrong. After the government cut a deal to sell land to nuclear contractor Badenwerk AG in early 1973, an even stronger coalition began to coalesce against the nuclear project in Wyhl.

Residents, farmers, hunters, and winegrowers worked with international groups of environmental and energy activists. They combined local outreach with expert research. Scientists from the University of Freiburg studied microclimates around the proposed nuclear site. They determined the water required to cool the reactor would draw down the water table and harm forests. At the same time, evaporation from the cooling towers could increase fog and impede local agriculture.

Opponents worked to publicize the issue and build a long-term, face-to-face movement. Organizer Walter Mossman would recount: "Many villagers, even those who don't read much, have been attending information meetings for years, reading books, distributing leaflets and stuffing them individually by the thousands into mailboxes (within a 50 km vicinity!), demonstrating, and sending out letters to the editor."[152]

This coincided with rising concern about nuclear power in other parts of Europe. In the community of Kaiseraugst, Switzerland, 100km south of Wyhl, another reactor had been proposed. In December 1973, opponents staged a week-long "trial squat" of that Swiss construction site.

Not all environmental justice struggles in the area were about nuclear energy. In the summer of 1974, in Marckolsheim, France—just across the border from Wyhl—a Munich-based company attempted to build a lead-processing factory. Lead, of course, is notoriously poisonous. After a series of protests, farmers, rural people, and allies took over the lead factory construction site—at one point blockading it with fifty tractors—and occupied it for months.

Organizers at Marckolsheim held a series of direct-action workshops and conducted joint organizing with their allies across the border in Wyhl. After an eight-month occupation, the Marckolsheim campaign was victorious—the company canceled their plans to build the factory.

Meanwhile, the long-term public mobilization effort in Wyhl was working. In 1974, some 90,000 people signed a statement against the nuclear reactor. Formal opposition was also declared by eight rural municipalities and some fifty different associations. A public poll by the Battelle Institute found that 75 percent of residents opposed the reactor.[153]

The government pushed forward anyway. They were required to hold public hearings about the proposed plant, which were organized in the summer of 1974.* However, opponents of the

---

* These hearings were a requirement of Germany's Atomic Energy Act of 1959.

plant soon found that the hearings were a sham: the government chaired the hearings, the government had proposed the project, and the government was even a partial owner of the nuclear contractor Badenwerk AG.

The hearings were conducted by an arrogant government official who cut off the microphones of residents who opposed the plant. Few citizens were permitted to speak. As a result, people became indignant and rowdy. Walter Mossman recalled: "The public did not restrict itself to listening during the two days of the discussion meeting. It revolted by chanting in chorus, heckling, and whistling whenever the official lies became too outrageous."[154]

A squadron of riot police lurked in the basement underneath the hearings; their presence was meant to keep the public in line.[155] After two days, regular people were fed up; they walked out of the hearings as a group, carrying a coffin with the words "the death of democracy."

In a further attempt to intimidate potential resisters, the government even sent a letter to residents threatening that the entire village of Wyhl could be expropriated if they opposed the project.[156]

Because of the perception that the public was being shut out of the process, more people and organizations—including the Protestant Church—coalesced in opposition to the government. The project became a threat not just to the environment or health but also to democracy. Project opponents publicly floated the idea of occupying the reactor site.[157] The government plowed forward anyway, issuing Badenwerk AG a permit to begin construction in early 1975. Police warned that any "trespasser" on the construction site would be fined 200 Marks per day.[158]

Opponents of the project filed legal challenges, staged protest marches, and participated in public hearings, but none of these were enough to stop the project. As construction began in early 1975, the movement against the reactor had one option left: direct action.

THE OCCUPATION

As construction began at the reactor site in Wyhl on February 17, 1975, residents saw what was happening and took collective action. The following day, a group of several hundred people, mostly residents, went to the fenced-off construction site where forest was being cut down.

It was not immediately clear that there would be an occupation. One citizen's association held a press conference about their leader change; another group leader said they had no plans to call for an occupation.[159]

However, the crowd eventually moved toward the site. When they saw the forest being destroyed, they knocked down the fence and climbed onto active construction equipment. Within minutes, the operation was shut down.

Despite the seeming spontaneity of the action, many of those present were well-prepared. Some of those who had escalated the action were activists from the struggle at Marckolsheim. Others had taken steps to prepare themselves, like Maria Köllhofer, a mother of five who lived nearby. When Köllhofer previously discussed the possibility of an occupation with her family, they had agreed that she should join the occupation on their behalf. Since then, she had kept a packed bag with warm clothing and provisions by her door.[160]

This diverse group of occupiers quickly set up trailers and tents on the side, and neighbors began to arrive with food and drink. Many participants had honed their logistical skills during the occupation at Marckolsheim.

The group of 150 people managed to hold the site for two days. On February 20, a force of 600 police attacked the demonstrators with ice-cold water cannons and arrested many of the occupiers. (The violence was a shock to many of the rural participants who were used to thinking of police as friends or neighbors.)

But by this point, the media had also arrived. Television coverage of farmers and residents being dragged through mud by police aired across the country.[161]

What had seemed like a regulatory issue in a quiet corner of the countryside suddenly became the center of national attention. Media coverage galvanized opposition to the plant and helped mobilize supporters across Germany and other parts of Europe.

Four days later, on February 23, 1975, opponents of the reactor rallied in force. This time, some 28,000 people arrived to demonstrate and begin a new occupation of the construction site.[162]

"When justice is turned into injustice," they declared, "to resist becomes an obligation."[163] Many kinds of people fulfilled that obligation: Wyhl residents, clergy, farmers, innkeepers, professors, hunters, environmentalists, doctors, teachers, winegrowers, students, and activists. It was a broad swath of people who cared about health, the land, and democratic process.

The police were caught off guard; only 250 officers were present. The police attacked demonstrators with their truncheons. However, the demonstrators did not retreat and were able to swarm around police, knock down fences, and take control of the construction site. When tens of thousands of people commit civil disobedience, it is nearly impossible to control them.

The occupiers used their momentum and the media spotlight to promote a national debate about nuclear power.

They built a kind of village on the proposed reactor site, including a community center dubbed the *Freundschaftshaus*, or "friendship house," which had room for hundreds of people. Historian Jens Ivo Engels writes: "From all over the Federal Republic, tens of thousands of protesters came, as on a pilgrimage to Wyhl. Through their presence at meetings and demonstrations, they articulated fears about nuclear energy and concern about ecological problems and the politics of energy-based economic development. Wyhl became a symbol of people's opposition to a state that was characterized as 'antidemocratic' and 'despotic.'"[164]

The movement hosted programs in the friendship house as part of a series called the Wyhl Forest Community College. Tens to hundreds of people attended each discussion, which covered everything from how a nuclear reactor worked to language and culture. The community college endured for a decade.

In addition to their ongoing recruitment and communications efforts, the occupiers took security measures to protect the site from incursions by police and corporate agents. The site was occupied or patrolled twenty-four hours a day by volunteer "guards," including local villagers. These "guards" often consisted of groups of women knitting.[165] Once the occupation was in place, several groups lived on the site—mostly students, young people, activists, and a handful of unemployed people.[166]

On March 21, 1975, the construction permit for the plant was withdrawn. This was a small victory, but Badenwerk AG appealed the decision. Occupiers were not ready to leave. Instead, they maintained the occupation through the summer of 1975. Thousands of people from across Europe visited the site, a living example of the power of civil disobedience.

The occupation would last nearly ten months in total. In the opening days of 1976, the government promised that construction would not resume until all complaints had been heard and the issue had worked its way through the courts. The occupiers withdrew from the site, knowing they had the public backing to return if necessary.

Finally, in March 1977, an administrative court announced its decision: there would be no nuclear reactor at Wyhl. The court claimed that the decision had been based on deficiencies in the nuclear plant design rather than the public outcry.

But opponents knew that they had won a real victory.

The proposed reactor site in Wyhl would become a nature reserve.

The convergence at Wyhl helped launch a new movement—
perhaps even several movements. Activist Petra Kelly visited the
Wyhl occupation (as she had visited the Green Bans in Australia)
and shortly thereafter co-founded the German Green Party. New
Green political parties proliferated around the world.

The Wyhl occupation gave momentum to campaigns for
democracy and environmental justice. Many people view it as
the symbolic birthplace of a modern movement against nuclear
power.

In the years that followed, a wave of occupations and major
struggles rippled across Europe. In the United States, organizers
inspired by the Wyhl campaign would stage even longer occupations as part of the Clamshell Alliance and the Abalone Alliance.

This was the hope of people like Marie-Reine Haug, who had
been an organizer in both the Marckolsheim and Wyhl occupations. She said: "The struggle against nuclear reactors must be a
chain reaction. One victory will trigger another."[167]

The victory at Wyhl would echo around the world for decades
to come. However, many of the anti-nuclear site fights that
followed did not succeed, in part because not all organizers understood the lessons of Wyhl.

VICTORY FACTORS AND THE AFTERMATH

How did this campaign against a nuclear plant win, even when
the government had chosen a municipality where they expected
to find the least resistance?

A big part of the answer has to do with the broad, diverse
opposition that organizers were able to develop. They used what
I've been calling full spectrum resistance, recruiting and mobilizing people from a variety of backgrounds and constituencies.
They synthesized their reasons for opposition—environmental

concerns, agricultural preservation, human health, and democracy—into a coherent and shared movement for environmental justice.

The campaign mobilized members to use diverse tactics, ranging from letters to the editor and legal challenges to civil disobedience.

The movement was particularly strong at recruitment and communications. From my experience as a farm organizer, I know that mobilizing people in rural areas can be much more challenging because of the geographical distances involved, and communications barriers were even more significant in the pre-internet era of the Wyhl campaign.

Opponents of the reactor began organizing immediately after it was announced and put in an enormous amount of legwork for many years, going door to door and speaking face-to-face with thousands of people.

This foundational organizing is a requirement for effective mass movements. However, television and mass media coverage of the struggle burst onto the airwaves after the occupation began. This sudden appearance in the news made the action appear ad hoc. Successful resistance on a large scale is almost never spontaneous.

After the victory, many people in other communities and struggles wanted to emulate Wyhl's success. However, organizers from the Wyhl campaign had difficulty convincing other activists of how much groundwork had been done to make the Wyhl campaign succeed.

Wyhl organizer Freia Hoffman said she was "forced to repeat time and again" that Wyhl succeeded because "a few people began the painstaking work of pointing out the dangers of atomic power plants, the patient work of organizing countless informational meetings, passing out umpteen-thousand flyers, collecting signatures, etc." Environmental Historian Stephen Milder notes: "It was this long history of patient effort, Hoffmann told whoever would listen, that had allowed for the successful occupation in 1975."[168]

When we look at a win that seems to come out of nowhere, it's easier to come to one of two misunderstandings: Either a) spontaneous uprisings can easily be called forth, or b) the circumstances of the uprising were so special that it can't be repeated.

In some communities fighting nuclear power, such misunderstandings led to a loss of morale. Freia Hoffman "heard that the example of Wyhl has led to resignation elsewhere." Some people in other parts of Germany assumed that the people of Wyhl were especially courageous and direct action simply wouldn't work in the rest of the country.[169]

On the other hand, it also caused some anti-nuclear activists who had visited Wyhl to try to jump straight to mass direct action without building a local grassroots foundation.

Milder explains: "It was not long, however, before these visitors discovered the difficulty of simply exporting 'Model Wyhl.' Years of alliance building and countless smaller actions had preceded the Wyhl occupation. The police, too, had learned from Wyhl and were better prepared to defend other construction sites. Thus, attempted occupations near the northern German towns of Brokdorf and Grondhe descended into pitched battles between protesters and police."

These occupations substantially delayed construction and required police to build elaborate, expensive fortifications. Defeating demonstrations of 100,000 people at Brokdorf required the biggest police operation in the history of West Germany, including the use of razor wire and armored personnel carriers.[170]

At Wahl, the number of participants and breadth of public support had deterred the police from large-scale attacks. However, at some other occupations, organizers had not been able to build the same kind of local support, and violent repression by police was successful in frightening off more moderate participants. Some occupations and protests later involved tens of thousands of dedicated resisters. But if militants are isolated from a broader base of support or forced to defend a fixed position from attack, the state can almost always mobilize overwhelming force to arrest or displace them.

That said, some struggles against specific reactors did succeed in various parts of Europe. A reactor was canceled at Kaiseraugst, Switzerland, thanks in part to direct action that had been happening there even before the occupation at Wyhl. A mass occupation at Kaiseraugst in April 1975 involved some 15,000 people and lasted four months. The government didn't give up but focused on influence operations, including constructing a two-story "information pavilion" for the planned reactor. But that empty building was blown up by underground militants in February of 1979.[171] By the time the Kaiseraugst project was finally abandoned (officially for "economic" reasons), it had cost the government well over a billion dollars.

Police repression against occupations at various reactor sites in Western Europe became extreme. In 1977, tens of thousands demonstrated against constructing a fast breeder reactor at Creys-Malville in France. And while the reactor would eventually be canceled, a demonstrator named Vital Michalon was killed by police in a campaign of violent repression.

In Wackersdorf, Bavaria, organizers campaigned through the 1980s against a nuclear fuel reprocessing plant. They used a wide variety of tactics, from peaceful demonstrations to music festivals to Molotov cocktails. The nuclear project was finally canceled in 1988 (after expenditures of over 1.3 billion dollars, not adjusted for inflation).[172] A solar cell factory and automobile recycler took over the location instead.

Even the "failed" site fights were critical in building long-term movements. As Milder notes, "concerns about nuclear energy became increasingly commonplace after Wyhl, drawing in an ever-wider cross-section of the population. In this sense, the grass-roots movement against reactors that took place along the Upper Rhine played a major part in making nuclear energy a hotly contested issue throughout Western Europe."[173]

A vigorous anti-nuclear movement continued for decades, limiting the proliferation of nuclear power. Indeed, that movement would ebb and surge in the decades to come, sometimes renewed especially after disasters like Chernobyl.

After the reactor meltdowns at Fukushima in 2011, the movement in Germany rose up again with vigorous protests and direct action. Shortly after, the German government pledged to shut down all German nuclear plants; as of 2023, that process was completed.

In the short term, the effects of this plan are mixed and somewhat complicated. Germany doesn't yet have enough renewable electricity capacity in place, and so the shutdown is leading to more burning of fossil fuels, particularly coal. This is not great from a climate change perspective.

However, global warming is already forcing some nuclear power plants in Europe to shut down periodically. Nuclear plants depend on effective cooling to function, and some recent heat waves have overwhelmed those cooling systems. Heat waves will only become more common as global warming progresses.[174]

In any case, Germany's nuclear plants closed. The work that the German anti-nuclear movement that launched at Wyhl is now complete.

The broader work of fighting climate change remains.

SEVEN

Standing Strong Against Nuclear Waste

SOUTH AUSTRALIA

2015–2017

A powerful alliance of Indigenous peoples, environmentalists, unions, and other groups organize to prevent a massive nuclear waste dump from being built on Indigenous land.

In 2015, the government of South Australia proposed creating a massive nuclear waste dump on Indigenous land that would accept radioactive waste from around the world.

The government wanted this for-profit project to import 138,000 tonnes of "high-level" waste—spent fuel from nuclear reactors, which remains dangerously radioactive for thousands of years. The government also wanted to store "intermediate" waste amounting to 390,000 cubic meters (that's approximately eleven times the volume of the reflecting pool at the National Mall in Washington, DC).

There was an immediate and powerful response from many different groups, but to understand what this movement did and why it won, we have to know a little about the history of nuclear weapons testing and the uranium mining industry in Australia.

NUCLEAR WEAPONS ON INDIGENOUS LAND

After the development of the atomic bomb during World War II, many countries initiated their own nuclear weapons programs. Newly developed bombs became much more powerful than the weapons dropped on Hiroshima and Nagasaki, and the nuclear powers used vast areas of "disposable" territory to test their new weapons.*

Such territory almost always meant the lands of Indigenous people. The United States government first tested its bombs on the lands of the Pueblo, Navajo, and Apache peoples (that is, New Mexico and Nevada). Later, they moved to Micronesian islands in the Pacific and Aleut territory in Alaska.

The Soviets tested their bombs mostly in Kazakhstan and Nenets territory in the Arctic.

The British also sought out testing grounds in the early 1950s. After being rejected by the government of Canada, they chose sites in South Australia, in areas occupied mainly by Indigenous people. The land chosen to be contaminated by atomic testing was used by Aboriginal people, as a Royal Commission would later report, for "hunting and gathering, for temporary settlements, for caretakership, and spiritual renewal."[175]

In typical colonial fashion, the government did not inform or consult Indigenous people about the use of their lands. Soldiers were sent to forcibly relocate Aboriginal peoples who lived near the blast sites.[176]

When the first atomic bombs went off at Emu Field in 1953, clouds of radioactive fallout drifted across Aboriginal territory.** Many people got sick. In some communities, up to half of all people may have died from the radioactive fallout.[177]

---

* This means that while nuclear bombs have been used against one nation (Japan) during war, many Indigenous nations and their territories have been bombed during times of "peace."
** These early nuclear test sites are still dangerously radioactive, even after a belated clean-up effort.

One survivor, a boy named Yami Lester, was permanently blinded by the fallout. However, he became a powerful advocate for Aboriginal rights and against the nuclear industry.

URANIUM POWER GROWS

In the decades after World War II, uranium mining and nuclear power became major industries in Australia. New mines were opened on Aboriginal land, and those mining operations produced piles of radioactive tailings. New atomic plants soon generated dangerous streams of waste.

At the same time, Aboriginal peoples and allies worked against those industries and for Aboriginal rights in general.

In the 1970s, a few military veterans of the early nuclear tests whom the state had sworn to secrecy risked arrest to become whistleblowers. The general public began to learn about testing sites that were still dangerously radioactive after decades and the illnesses and deaths they caused.

Aboriginal people and military veterans of the tests reported chronic illnesses from blindness to cancer. So many stillbirths and severe birth defects occurred that a "baby cemetery" was set up near Woomera.

In the 1980s, a Royal Commission investigated the British Atomic Bomb tests. Aboriginal people and environmentalists used mass organizing and direct action against uranium mining companies. Organizing into large movements like the Coalition for a Nuclear-Free Australia, they organized blockades of uranium mines and disrupted mining company offices.

The anti-nuclear movement in Australia became increasingly powerful. It was also supported by the Green Party (one of the earliest in the world), which had representatives elected at every level of government.

In the late twentieth century, several other nuclear dumps were proposed. Many were defeated, thanks in large part to the work of Aboriginal peoples. One particular dump proposed in South Australia was defeated in 2004 thanks to a women-led campaign called *Irati Wanti* (which translates to "the poison, leave it").

The existence of these recent models for action clarified the movement's strategic options and boosted recruitment.

THE SOUTH AUSTRALIA NUCLEAR WASTE DUMP

By the time the government of South Australia decided to create a new nuclear waste dump in 2015, movement organizers already had several key factors in their favor:

* They had built a strong *culture of resistance* over decades.

* They had experience with a *diversity of tactics*—not just polite advocacy but also blockades and disruption.

* They had a *history of building diverse movements* with many organizations and people from many backgrounds.

* They had *strong organizing skills* and had developed their *movement capacities* for communication, fundraising, and other areas.

Decades of hard work and dedication had put the movement in a strong position to oppose proponents of a nuclear waste dump.

When the government of South Australia announced the 2015 plan, it also initiated a multi-million-dollar pro-nuclear propaganda campaign called "Know Nuclear." It carried out a series of "consultations" about the proposed dump. Aboriginal people criticized the consultations for being closed, secretive, inadequate, and phony.

The movement's response to the announcement was immediate and began with a variety of awareness-raising tactics. Organizers established or revived local groups and held meetings and info nights to discuss nuclear issues in their communities, including casual events like "politics at the pub."

They held press conferences, made posters, t-shirts, and badges, and reached out on social media. They distributed research reports and fact sheets to counter government disinformation. They were able to make the human and environmental stakes clear.

Movement organizers also celebrated past victories and models for action. They promoted the *Irati Wanti* campaign (which had won in 2004) by staging a photo exhibition and publishing a book called *Talking Straight Out*.

Once they established and strengthened their movement's foundation through outreach and awareness-raising, activists turned to mobilization. In May 2016, they announced a formal coalition called the "No Dump Alliance," backed by Aboriginal groups, unions, churches, and environmentalists.

They held anti-nuclear walks to bring people out to uranium mining areas. In July, anti-nuclear activists held a three-day convergence and training camp called "The Lizard Bites Back" and staged a blockade of the Olympic Dam uranium mine.

Meanwhile, "Traditional Owners"—Indigenous people as recognized by Australian Law—issued joint statements against uranium mining, nuclear reactors, and nuclear waste dumps on their lands.

The campaign continued to gain momentum through the summer of 2016. The No Dump Alliance organized a postcard and petition campaign that gathered 35,000 signatures—a substantial achievement in a country with a population of 24 million.

Thousands of people marched in the streets for a Day of Action on October 15, 2016, exactly sixty-three years after the first atomic bomb test at Emu Junction.

Having established an increasingly powerful and multi-faceted movement, some began advocating for escalation.

An opinion piece in the Australian newspaper *Red Flag* called for workers to take direct action:

> In the wake of French nuclear tests in the early 1970s, unions such as the Waterside Workers Federation put black bans on the export of uranium.
>
> If our side is going to win, we need to keep mobilizing thousands in protest for as long as nuclear waste is on the table. Most importantly, unions can wield their industrial strength. Projects of this scale require the cooperation of innumerable workers. If dock workers refuse to unload canisters of waste from ships, if transport workers refuse to move waste from shore to site, if construction workers refuse to build a dump and if teachers refuse to allow the government's pro-nuclear tripe to be taught to students, the whole project will fall apart.[178]

Many Aboriginal people had been clear all along that they would use direct action to stop the project. Arabunna Elder Kevin Buzzacott warned: "To the South Australian government, to the federal government, to the mining giants—don't worry about trying to put the waste dump here. Because you'll be wasting your money. We'll be out there trying to stop it."[179] Sue Coleman-Haseldine, another survivor of the 1950s bomb tests, promised: "We will fight it anywhere."[180]

VICTORY

With a mass movement in the streets and on the land, things began to shift in government. The premier of South Australia created a "Citizens' Jury" on the dump. By the end of that process, two-thirds of the Jury rejected the nuclear dump "under any circumstances." In June 2017, the premier admitted that the plan was dead.

Hoping to prevent another "Know Nuclear" public relations campaign, the Green Party introduced a bill to ban public money from being spent "to encourage or finance nuclear waste storage facilities"—it passed.

The defeat of the nuclear waste dump in South Australia is well worth celebrating and studying.

The movement's *fast response* was a key factor. Because they fought so hard while the nuclear waste dump was still in the planning stage, they prevented the government from initiating construction. The movement was able to seize and keep the initiative.

Their *communications and messaging* were also very clear and not *abstract*. The movement against the nuclear dump emphasized the tangible harm a dump could impose. They were able to do this in part through the leadership of Aboriginal people like Yami Lester, whose words and blindness reminded supporters of the real danger of nuclear colonialism.

Lastly, *radical flanking* was at work in the campaign, thanks to the threat of escalating direct action and the uncompromising stance of dump opponents. Governments immensely dislike dealing with direct action, which is disruptive and unpredictable, and would much rather funnel popular discontent into well-managed and orderly "consultations." However, opponents of the dump refused to fall into this trap and were prepared to use many different tactics.

As a result, the governing Labor Party was forced to backpedal throughout the campaign in a failing attempt to maintain control, first by initiating its "Citizens' Jury" and then by canceling the project. Radical flanking also happened in Parliament because of the presence of the Green Party, which has long opposed uranium mining, nuclear waste, and nuclear weapons and which draws much of its support from disillusioned Labor supporters who feel that the traditional union party has slid too much to the right.

All these factors together made for a powerful and ultimately victorious campaign—something we can all learn from.

HOTELLING'S LAW

Radical flanking can be a powerful force in social movements. It was also at play *within* the government in South Australia when the Green Party outflanked the governing Liberals to help force the cancellation of the nuclear waste dump.

However, radical flanking doesn't always work within government, and is particularly difficult when there are two dominant political parties. The reason has to do with an observation called "Hotelling's Law."

The notion came from Harold Hotelling, a statistician and economic theorist. He observed that competing retailers often make very similar products, even when differentiated products might seem more sensible—and observation that would also apply to politics.

Hotelling's Law works like this: imagine there are only two ice-cream carts on a long boardwalk. It's a hot day, and everyone wants ice cream. If we think in terms of common sense, we could space out the ice cream trucks to cover the whole boardwalk:

First: ice cream vendors evenly spaced

In that case, anyone who wants ice cream would have to travel a fairly short distance. In practice, however, if one ice cream vendor moves toward the middle, they can poach customers from the middle section. Meanwhile, they are still the closest vendor for customers at their end of the boardwalk.

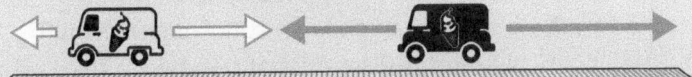

Then: moving toward center to poach customers

If one ice cream vendor moves toward the middle, the other vendor may do the same to keep their share of the customers. A few moves later, the situation looks like this:

Finally: both vendors converge at centre

From the perspective of the ice-cream *eaters*, this is incredibly inconvenient. Anyone at the ends of the boardwalk will have to walk the greatest possible distance to get ice cream. But from the perspective of a selfish ice cream vendor, it makes a certain kind of sense.

The same thing can happen in a nation dominated by a two-party political system, like the United States. Ostensibly liberal and conservative parties may inch toward each other in an attempt to poach swing voters from the other side until their actual policies differ very little.* Voters with political views further from the "average" can settle for whichever party is marginally closer to the voter's perspective.

The boardwalk example applies if there are two ice cream carts. But if you add a third, the pattern breaks down, and vendors may spread themselves out again to avoid being "pinched" out of the center.

Something similar can occur in countries with multi-party political systems—like Australia—where a third or fourth party can have an outsized impact.

---

* Of course, this convergence can also be the result of corporate donations and lobbyists, since corporate donors usually want any governing party to adopt business-friendly, neoliberal policies.

1984 DAY OF ACTION FOR A NUCLEAR-FREE AUSTRALIA

Australia has a long history of direct action against uranium mining and the nuclear industry. Consider this report from a *single day* of action on October 31, 1984, as reported in the anti-nuclear newspaper *Chain Reaction*:[181]

Members of the Coalition for a Nuclear-Free Australia (CNFA) held an Australia-wide day of action on 31 October 1984. Opposition to Roxby Downs did not end with the blockade of the mine in August and September but carries on in each capital city Tom Worsnop and Maz Kerin report.

Actions involved people from six states hindering work in the offices of the two partners in the giant Roxby Downs uranium mine—British Petroleum (BP) and Western Mining Corporation (WMC). Each group delivered some radioactive material collected from the Roxby tailings dam (evaporation pond) during the [previous] blockade, so giving management the task of disposing of their mine by-products personally. . . .

In **Adelaide** the protestors entered RMS's office and delivered the radioactive sample with the intention of staying by being locked in the building but they were quickly kicked out. There was a gathering of supporters outside. All the Adelaide media were present but there was no press coverage.

In **Canberra**, protesters went into the BP office, where only two people work, and delivered tailings. Activists regularly visit this office and effectively frustrate BP's operations.

In **Sydney**, two people managed to get on to the roof of BP house, dropped a banner over the side which read "BP—the Quiet Deceiver." They delivered and left tailings. Six were arrested in the office, others leafleted the street outside.

Ten people entered WMC's office in **Perth** and left tailings. Seven people were arrested after chaining themselves to the doors.

In **Brisbane** six people entered BP house and superglued tailings to the desk. They were arrested straightaway. Four of them were carried across the street to the police station. When the media turned up the remaining two protectors were taken out the back and delivered across the road in a police van.

In **Melbourne** nine people entered WMC's offices in Collins Street posing as student teachers doing an assignment. Seven chained themselves to the office doors and superglued the locks. They sang protest songs and disrupted the office. Sixteen police were called in wielding 90 cm bolt-cutters. They succeeded in cutting through all the padlocks but couldn't break a "kryptonite" bike lock which remained on one of the doors. Seven of the protestors were arrested and charged with willful trespass.

EIGHT

Umbergaon Port

A group of fishers and villagers stop the construction of a megaport that threatens their land and livelihood, defeating both the Indian government and a powerful transnational corporation. However, not everyone survives to see the day of victory.

Gujarat is the westernmost state in India, and its southern coast is home to dozens of fishing villages. People have been fishing there for thousands of years. According to the late Thomas Kocherry, once chair of India's National Fishworkers Forum, they've gotten very good at it: "Over the centuries, the fisher people have amassed a vast fund of knowledge about the resources in their immediate vicinity and have developed a variety of technologies tailored to specific ecological niches along the coast. This accounts for the immense diversity of artisanal fishing techniques in the country, the hallmark of which has been their ecological sophistication rather than an orientation towards quick monetary gain."[182]

However, during the intense capitalist globalization of the late 1990s, quick monetary gain was the goal of both corporations and governments alike. To increase the gross domestic product and enrich a handful of corporations, the Indian government was willing to sacrifice traditional livelihoods and the ecological integrity of coastal India.

New "Special Economic Zones" were created for industrial production—places where the normal rules didn't apply. Coastal regions were snapped up for tourist resorts and privatized beaches. Hydroelectric dams and water pollution devastated fish habitats. Mass-scale shrimp farming took over coastal areas at the same time that industrial fishing was displacing more sustainable, traditional methods.

Shrimp farming and industrial fishing go together, as Thomas Kocherry explained: "Fresh fish caught by industrial vessels is converted into fish meal for the production of shrimp. Ten thousand tonnes of fish that would have been available for the common man are converted into fish meal to produce 1,000 tonnes of shrimp that only the rich can afford to buy."[183]

With these changes, fish populations declined steeply. A handful of people got rich at the expense of traditional communities and the planet.

That was the context in 1999 when the Indian government—without consulting the people who lived in Gujarat or considering the impact on land or water—decided that Gujarat would be the site of an enormous port complex. The $300 million-dollar megaport was to be built by Unocal on the southern tip of Gujarat.

THE MEGAPORT

Unocal had no specific expertise in maritime engineering. But it did have experience making a profit by exploiting humans and destroying the environment. Unocal has been at the forefront of violent capitalist globalization for decades. In Afghanistan in the 1990s, Unocal worked with the Taliban and allegedly supported Taliban efforts to control the country so that the corporation could build a pipeline.[184] Villagers in Burma alleged that Unocal's presence resulted in rape, murder, and forced labor. Unocal was such a notorious polluter and abuser of employees in its home state of California that in 1994, some thirty different organizations petitioned the attorney general to revoke Unocal's corporate charter.[185]

When the new port in Gujarat was announced, a report from the Indian People's Tribunal on Environmental and Human Rights (IPT) warned that the project would destroy the livelihoods of 75,000 people in twenty-one villages.[186]

In February 1999, villagers in Gujarat found out about the planned megaport and formed a group called Kinara Bachao Sangharsh Samiti (KBSS)—the Save the Coast Action Committee.

The Samiti eventually represented some fifty villages and chose Lt. Colonel Pratap Save to be their president. Save spoke English, Hindi, and Gujarati and had recently retired from the military to return to his hometown to enjoy a peaceful life working on his family farm.*

When the Samiti began organizing, they did not begin by approaching the federal government. Instead, they focused on grassroots organizing. They raised awareness, educated their neighbors, and got local governments to pass resolutions opposing the port.

In doing this, the Samiti was able to draw on Gujarat's long history of resistance. Gujarat only exists as a separate state because Gujarati-speaking peoples organized for years to win their own homeland.

The Samiti had been organizing for over a year when government workers showed up to start surveying the site of the proposed megaport.

---

* Save's father had been a "freedom fighter" in the Indian independence movement, according to journalist Anosh Malekar.

On the morning of April 7, 2000, some women in the village of Umbergaon saw about 200 members of the State Reserve Police setting up tents on land that was privately owned by villagers. The State Reserve Police guard important government-owned infrastructure like power plants, ports, and dams.

The women alerted others, and the community learned that the police had come to ensure that a survey of the megaport site could proceed. The villagers promptly organized a *dharna* (a nonviolent sit-in) at the police encampment, singing protest songs against the port and the incursion onto their land.

The Samiti's president arrived at the protest site that same evening. He and other members of the Samiti met with the commandant of the State Reserve Police and local officials to demand that the government cancel the survey and the police remain peaceful.

Local officials went to the site where about 500 villagers were demonstrating and shouting slogans. Instead of ordering the police to withdraw, however, the officials ordered them to attack the demonstrators.

Police used batons and tear gas to disperse the protesters. Even after demonstrators had left the police encampment, journalist Anosh Malekar told me, "State Reserve Police and local police continued to unleash terror the entire night as they roamed or patrolled the village streets armed with batons and hit anyone they came across. I met some of the injured men, women, and even children as young as twelve years old."

Malekar added: "It was very clear that the protesters were nonviolent and were only trying to prevent the survey through slogan shouting and a sit-in, which are democratic means well-known and accepted across India for decades. The government, its officials, and security personnel claimed otherwise. But I did not come across a single injured security personnel, nor could the government give us evidence of any violent act like stone pelting, use of sticks, metal bars or any arms by the protesting villagers."

The police arrested many activists from the Samiti. In the middle of the night, police went to Lt. Colonel Save's house and arrested him on trumped-up charges, alleging that he started a riot.

The police continued their campaign of intimidation and violence against the imprisoned Samiti members. The police beat Save so severely that he died from his injuries. Authorities claimed that Save died from "natural causes."

Malekar suggested to me that the violent repression of a peaceful protest and the death of Save "clearly hints at a not-so-secret plan by the government to terrorize and cause fear among the villagers, with the ultimate aim of defeating the opposition to the port project." This would be consistent with how Unocal and partner governments have behaved around the world.

Though wounded and grieving, the Samiti did not back down. Instead, they escalated. They engaged with new allies and reached out to other organizations. They even invited high-ranking retired military officers to visit them and to speak out on the murder of a veteran by the government.

The Samiti set up a people's commission to investigate Save's death. They also organized a number of *pad yatras* (traveling foot marches) through the villages around Gujarat. The marchers included activists, students, villagers, and retired teachers.[187] As they traveled, they stopped in villages to hold public meetings and to inform and mobilize the residents.

On August 15, 2000, the marches converged in Umbergaon for a flag-hosting ceremony attended by 20,000 people.[188]

It worked. The government abandoned their plan and Unocal lost the lucrative contract. They lost a leader, but the small fishers and farmers of Gujarat won their campaign.

WHY THEY WON

Several key factors contributed to the community victory, including:

* ⋆   Grassroots organizing and local gradualism
* ⋆   Diverse tactics
* ⋆   Refusal to back down in the face of repression
* ⋆   A culture of resistance

Movement-building takes time and much of that must happen face-to-face. Good grassroots organizing makes movements resistant to "decapitation attacks." Governments often try to repress effective movements by imprisoning or even murdering their leaders, and the Samiti's preparations included lining up leaders who were ready to step up if they were needed.

Local gradualism—the process of building up movements at the local scale before moving up to federal or national levels—was also used effectively by the Samiti.

The movement against the megaport also employed a variety of tactics, from awareness-raising meetings and marches to legal challenges and sit-ins.

Critical, too, was their sheer persistence. Even when faced with violent repression, the movement refused to stop or to give in. Instead, the people kept up their campaign, and even escalated the mobilization.

Lastly, the culture of resistance in Gujarat made it easier to mobilize people to action, because ordinary people already understood the importance of protest.

As noted, the state of Gujarat only exists because of a social movement demanding a state for Gujarat-speaking people. There was a youth movement in 1974 which forced the removal of a corrupt chief minister.* That movement was so strong that its name, Navnirman, is literally synonymous with mass protest in Gujarat; for example, "If government does not fulfill our demands, we will create another Navnirman."[189] There had been strong movements against government emergency powers (1975–1977), and for farmers (1986–2004).

Research scholar Mukesh Semwal explains that these movements strengthened a popular belief in *Jan Shakti*, or people power, explaining that participants came to understand "people power can build or destroy any power on Earth." This confidence in common people's involvement in the political process, Semwal said, helped remove a corrupt high-level official and gave a boost to movement organizing all over India.[190]

Fisher people were very active in mass protest and direct action during these struggles. In 1976, in Tuticorin, small-scale fishermen used fire to destroy eleven trawlers, and in 1989, there were mass marches—mostly of women—to protect waters and stop exploitation.[191]

The victory against the mega port in 2000 helped to fortify a culture of resistance, including small victories won through a hunger strike by Father Thomas Kocherry and mass action in 2008 against coastal development.

When we nourish resistance, we build on a deep history of successful organizing and establish the foundation for future wins.

* * *

I'll be honest—I considered leaving out the story of the struggle against Umbergaon Port. It wasn't as thoroughly documented as other stories, lacked photographs, and was more difficult to

---

* A chief minister in India is the elected head of a state government, analogous to a state governor in the US, or a provincial premier in Canada.

research. I wasn't able to directly interview participants because most of the organizers are now dead and left few written records of their struggle.

And yet, their struggle was real and meaningful. It made a lasting difference, even though it wasn't the subject of books or social media posts.

To retell this story is a way to amplify unsung victories and ensure that the successful struggle against Umbergaon Port remains in the historical record.

This campaign is what I think of as a *phantom victory*. It was a real victory, and yet few records of it remain. How can we learn from victories we do not know about? How can we honor the sacrifices of those whose names have been forgotten?

Of course, there exist innumerable social movement successes that were never recorded in writing. We live in a curious historical moment, in which billions of gigabytes are recorded each day. Yet, the very victories that could inform and nourish us are washed away in a digital mist.

The memory loss of movement victories is a real problem, and—thanks in part to our increasingly digital world—more pervasive and insidious than might be apparent.

I've been writing nonfiction books for twenty years now. In that time, the works I cite have (by necessity) shifted from mostly print sources to mostly digital or internet sources.

But these digital sources can be even more ephemeral than human memory. When I reviewed the bibliography of *Full Spectrum Resistance* just before its release in print, I was shocked by how many of the sources I'd linked to were simply gone. Local news stories, radical communiques, profiles of activists—small journalism of all kinds—had just disappeared.

This phenomena—known as "bit rot" or "link rot"—was especially bad for small or independent news outlets. These are exactly the sorts of places that give better or more detailed coverage of social movements and grassroots sources.*

In my time as a nonfiction author, this phenomenon of bit rot has gotten dramatically worse. And it seems to be accelerating, worsened by the following trends:

1) *The loss of small and independent media projects, like Indymedia,* from the early days of the web. So many important reports and communiques were posted to sites like these.[192]

2) *Corporate consolidation of news media* and the continuing loss of independent media and print media. I worked as a newspaper columnist and freelance journalist for five years with a network of local papers in my region. One day, however, newspaper staff showed up to find the doors of their office locked. Two major news corporations in Canada had cut a secret deal to buy each other's papers. The websites were also shuttered, the archives gone. On more than one occasion, I have tried to cite or share the journalism I have written, only to find that it has vanished.

3) *A shift from open internet to social networks,* with their own internal and unpredictable search functions, opaque algorithms, and unaccountable censorship and shadowbans. These social networks have extracted attention and advertising dollars that would previously have paid journalists, where governments have tried to level the playing field for media, as in Canada, platforms like Facebook and Instagram responded by simply blocking news from their services altogether—essentially limiting users only to information sources that *weren't* fact-checked.

4) The *widespread "enshittification" of social media,* like the micro-blogging site formerly known as Twitter, toward barely functional, Nazi-friendly cesspools.

---

* If you are a journalist or writer, I strongly recommend that you save all copies of important digital sources to your own backup system! I have relied on this often, but I've also been saved many times by the people who created the invaluable Internet Archive at archive.org.

5) Those existing trends now combine with *emerging threats to truth via Generative "AI" and Large Language Models*, like ChatGPT, controlled by large corporations. Accurate and independent sources of information on grassroots movements will become even harder to find and verify as the internet is flooded with auto-generated articles that are either dubious or entirely fabricated.

Social movement wins, at the best of times, can be ephemeral in the public consciousness. All the factors above make it even more important to remember, study, and celebrate victories.

That's why I decided to include the story of the struggle at Umbergaon Port, not *despite* its lack of print documentation but because of it.

NINE

Phantom Victories, Pipelines, and Gas Plants

ACROSS CANADA

2012–PRESENT

Loose coalitions of Indigenous peoples, environmentalists, and allies organize against fossil fuel pipelines and gas-burning power plants. Some struggles fail and are remembered; some succeed, but disappear from popular memory.

LINE 9

A social movement's loss can be prolonged and dramatic. When a conflict is visibly dragged out, it generates a written record: news stories, arrest records, court transcripts, obituaries.

But a decisive win—one that follows our principle of preemption—might leave very little record whatsoever.

Allow me a few examples, beginning with the contrast between two anti-pipeline struggles—one of which was ultimately successful and one which was not.

In 2012, Enbridge Inc.—the most profitable company in Canada at the time—decided it wanted to reverse the direction of an oil pipeline called Line 9.*

---

* Line 9 consisted of two segments: Line 9A and Line 9B. Line 9B is much longer and its reversal was strongly contested. When I refer to Line 9 in this passage, I'm specifically writing about Line 9B.

Line 9, which ran from Montreal, Quebec, to Sarnia, Ontario, had previously been used to import crude oil from Atlantic ports to refineries in Sarnia. In the decades since its construction, however, the economics of oil had changed dramatically. Canada had shifted from an oil importer to an oil-exporting petrostate.

This was driven largely by the exploitation of the tar sands in northern Alberta, which was (and remains) ecologically ruinous. Barrel for barrel, oil production from the tar sands emitted some four times as much carbon dioxide as the extraction of traditional crude.

Because these fossil fuels were mixed with sand in the form of bitumen (rather than traditional liquid crude), their extraction involved stripping away the living ecosystems above (the "overburden"). Vast amounts of energy were used to heat fresh water that could wash tar from the sand, along with chemical cracking agents that would liquefy the bitumen into a form that could be transported by pipeline instead of a dump truck.

The contaminated water was held in "tailings ponds"—closer to lakes in size. Migrating birds who landed in the ponds were frequently killed in enormous numbers. The destruction of the landscape went alongside air and water pollution that directly harmed communities of Indigenous people who continue to live in their traditional territory—albeit on smaller reserves and without the sovereignty and autonomy that is their right.

This context is important for many reasons: it partly explains *why* Enbridge was so profitable. Not only was the corporation capitalizing on a colonial oil rush on land that had been stolen through a generations-long genocide. It also externalized its costs in the form of harm to birds, the land, Indigenous communities, and all future generations (in the form of massive greenhouse gas emissions).

The chemistry of the process, too, is relevant. The thick, liquefied bitumen produced from the tar sands was very different from traditional crude. It was acidic and abrasive and had to be pumped at higher pressures. In other words, it was a very poor match for the aging, rusty conduit that was Line 9.

Enbridge wanted to reverse the direction of Line 9, fill it with bitumen, and pump that bitumen to Atlantic ports for export. The safety of those who lived alongside the pipeline was a major concern, and with good reason—Line 9 had a twin pipeline in Michigan that had already experienced a disaster.

Line 6B—which ran from Griffith, Indiana to Sarnia, Ontario, through the US state of Michigan—had been built around the same time as Line 9 and to the same specifications. Like Line 9, it was built with a wall much thinner than recent pipelines—a mere quarter of an inch thick). It was likewise operated by Enbridge.

On July 25, 2010, Line 6B ruptured and spilled more than a million gallons of diluted bitumen into the Kalamazoo River. (The cost of cleanup, initially estimated at $5 million, would eventually cost more than $1.2 billion.)

Hence, in 2012, when Enbridge announced it planned to reverse the flow of the pipeline and fill it with liquified bitumen, community opposition arose immediately.

A coalition formed, led by Indigenous organizers—especially young activists like Vanessa Gray of Aamjiwnaang First Nation. Nonprofit organizations like Toronto-based Environmental Defence participated in the campaign, along with many smaller grassroots groups.

With some dear comrades, I helped form a group called decLine 9 to organize in our region of eastern Ontario.

Our loose coalition undertook several approaches at once. Part of the struggle was rooted in long-term environmental justice organizing. The fossil fuel industry had particularly afflicted the Anishinaabe community of Aamjiwnaang. Much of their traditional territory had been taken over by oil refineries. The city of

Decline 9 developed a comedic piece of radical theatre entitled "The Spill Experts" which was performed at various a community events to build public knowledge. In this still image from a recording, a "scientist" from Enbridge "cleans up" an oil spill by mopping it up with a baby duckling, as a horrified "PR expert" (the author) looks on.

Sarnia, which occupies their lands, is at the intersection of several major pipeline routes, including Line 9. The area—dubbed "Chemical Valley"—has long been a hotspot for pollution, degraded air quality, and cancers.

People in the community of Aamjiwnaang suffered the most. They were surrounded by industry and had little historical political leverage due to environmental racism.

Another part of the coalition focused on raising awareness about safety. Because Line 9 was so old, many cities and neighborhoods in Ontario had been built around it. The pipeline ran less than a meter from a subway station in Toronto through vulnerable nature areas and communities, including next to an old folk's home.[193] * However, many people living next to it didn't even realize it was there or the potential threat it posed.

Another aspect of the campaign focused on climate, the environment, and the negative impacts of tar sands exploitation.

To reverse the pipeline, Enbridge needed approval from the National Energy Board, which regulates pipelines and similar infrastructure. The National Energy Board (NEB) held public hearings in cities along the route of the pipeline. Community groups and experts could apply to become "intervenors" at these hearings, giving statements to the board and providing evidence for their case.

Participation in this process was extremely labor intensive. We had to review thousands of pages of maps, documentation, and reports to understand what to say within the NEB's highly technical context.

The question arose repeatedly—should we try to interrupt or disrupt the hearings? Ultimately, coalition members decided that the arguments of intervenors should be heard. This was not a universal opinion. Some organizers believed that the NEB hearings were essential for educating the public and intervening in the political process. Others thought the NEB would approve the pipeline regardless of public input, as was their habit. However, Indigenous intervenors wanted to speak. To encourage that and maintain unity of the campaign, we decided not to interrupt the hearings.

Yet, after more than a year of review, the NEB rubber-stamped the pipeline. This was their general practice, and many expected it from the beginning.

---

* This became especially pertinent after the disaster at Lac-Mégantic, Quebec, in 2013. A train full of oil tankers had been parked for the night on a long, inclined section of track. Left unattended in the middle of the night, the train's brakes failed, and the train rolled back down the incline, accelerating until it derailed next to an old folk's home. The derailed tanker cars caught fire. The intense blaze killed forty-seven people, and destroyed much of the town.

The struggle didn't end there. To the contrary, it escalated.

A legal challenge to the pipeline, launched by Chippewas of the Thames First Nation, would make it all the way to Canada's Supreme Court. (After years of legal work, that court would eventually side with the pipeline company.)

There were waves of protests and nonviolent direct action at many locations along the route.

Organizers also coordinated across the province to arrange larger-scale actions to prevent the pipeline from being reversed. The pipeline was already in the ground, but its pumping stations (located at regular intervals along the route) had to be overhauled and heavy machinery replaced.

When one of those pumping stations was being renovated in June 2013, a coordinated group of activists from across the province took over the site and stopped work for a week. I was part of a group that set up a protest camp with food, community events, and collective decision-making. The joy and power of that time are among my most enduring memories of that campaign.

Police pressure and the risk involved eventually outweighed the strategic benefits of occupying the site. Most people left, though some locked down at the gate. Police arrested eighteen people.

There were other direct actions, too, with more arrests. Once the pipeline started pushing oil again, activists disrupted it by using manual emergency safety valves to cut off the flow.

Ultimately, the Enbridge corporation got what it wanted, and Line 9 was reversed. With most of the infrastructure already in the ground, we had known from the beginning that it would be a hard campaign, with fewer opportunities to directly obstruct pipeline construction.

Our group took time to debrief—something that I strongly recommend that all groups do after a campaign, regardless of the outcome.

As part of the debrief, we ranked the actions by how we perceived their impact and our desire to do something similar again.

Interestingly, even though the occupation of the pumping station was a "failure," members of our group rated it as our favorite action, the sort of thing we wanted to do more of. (It helped that we avoided arrest and jail in the aftermath.)

The campaign against Line 9 did *not* lead to the victory we were aiming for—stopping the pipeline from being reversed. Despite that—and in a way we weren't fully aware of—we did achieve other victories. We had built anti-pipeline networks across a wide geographic area. We built popular awareness about the dangers and injustices of pipelines and the fossil fuel industry. We had trained ourselves and others in the tactics of direct action.

We had shown a willingness to take risks to block or impede pipeline construction. For those who had followed along with the campaign, we had exposed the National Energy Board's inability to meaningfully challenge or regulate pipeline companies.

We can learn a lot from defeat. But I'd much rather learn from victory.

ENERGY EAST

At the very beginning of this book, I wrote of the often successful attempts to block pipelines connecting with the Alberta tar sands. Indigenous-led direct action campaigns successfully stopped Enbridge's Northern Gateway pipeline (which would have run west to the Pacific Ocean) and the Keystone XL pipeline (which would have run south, connecting indirectly to Texas and the Gulf of Mexico).

Those pipelines were blocked entirely. Meanwhile, other Indigenous campaigns were delaying and threatening pipeline projects like Trans Mountain and the Dakota Access Pipeline.

Desperate to find a way to export petroleum stolen from the

lands of Indigenous nations like the Dene and Cree, TransCanada Energy proposed an entirely new pipeline: Energy East.

Announced in 2013, the pipeline was intended to run from Alberta through Saskatchewan, Manitoba, Ontario, and Quebec to reach an Atlantic port in New Brunswick.

Like Line 9, Energy East had to be approved through a series of hearings at the National Energy Board. Hearings were scheduled for 2016 in cities along the planned pipeline route: Saint John, Montreal, Quebec City, and Kingston.

This bureaucratic process was very familiar to us. Intervenors began to register to participate, dusted off their slides, and prepared to make the same arguments as before.

And yet, something fundamental had changed. The collective attitude of activists in the loose anti-pipeline coalition had changed. People knew what the outcome of the NEB process would be, and they knew that the National Energy Board would rubber-stamp whatever industry proposed.

At the same time, all the formal arguments affirming Indigenous sovereignty, environmental justice, and climate protection had already been made in the previous series of NEB hearings. The new round of hearings no longer served a strategic purpose for us, so we decided to disrupt them.

In Kingston, we planned to sneak into the hearings and use banners and noise-makers to grind proceedings to a halt. However, our comrades were so effective in disrupting hearings in Montreal that those planned for Kingston and other cities were canceled.

The writing was on the wall. TransCanada knew it would be in for a long, expensive fight—that to push forward, it would have to risk spending billions of dollars on a project it might never complete. The economic context of the process, TransCanada said, had changed. In the face of sustained public protest, TransCanada caved in and abandoned its plans for Energy East.

LINE 9 AND ENERGY EAST

From the beginning, the strategic challenges and possibilities of the Line 9 and Energy East pipelines differed significantly.

While we had few points of physical intervention for Line 9—it was already buried in the ground—that was not the case for Energy East. They planned to build a new pipeline, which required years of regulatory approvals to secure easements, excavation, pipe-laying, pumping and monitoring stations, and so on.

Each of those phases would have provided opportunities for disruption. Every mile of the proposed route was a potential space for protest, struggle, and occupation. The route was so long that it would have been impossible to defend against a dedicated movement.

The fight against Energy East was a decisive victory. By contrast, it might be tempting to call the fight against Line 9 a failure.

But that would be simplistic, misleading, and ultimately wrong.

Movements achieve their stated change goal in decisive victories. Viewed strictly by decisive outcomes, our Energy East campaign was a success, but our Line 9 campaign was not.

And yet, I'm not sure we would have won the fight against Energy East if we hadn't previously waged a campaign against Line 9. We certainly wouldn't have won it as quickly or as easily.

Line 9 was a shaping and sustaining win. Energy East wouldn't have been stopped without the innumerable protests, speaking events, legal challenges, and direct actions that had been arrayed against it over many years.

Ironically, there is an odd disparity in the public imagination between Line 9 and Energy East. Many people remember the struggle against Line 9. I still get emails about it and run into people I recognize from that campaign nearly a decade ago.

But almost everyone—unless they were directly involved—has forgotten that Energy East was ever proposed.

Energy East became a kind of phantom victory, largely forgotten, while our memories of the Line 9 defeat live on. Indeed, more than just our memories of the Line 9 struggle remain.

There are countless newspaper articles about the campaign, thousands and thousands of pages of documentation, arrest records, and court transcripts. I still have banners, T-shirts, and a lab coat I wore to portray an Enbridge "expert" during a street theater action. That lab coat and a stuffed "duckling" from the same show still smell of the fake crude oil we made from molasses, cocoa powder, and vegetable oil.

Victories don't just become phantom victories automatically. In some sense, they only become phantom victories when we fail to celebrate, remember, and learn from them.

On that note, there is another recent movement victory I want to celebrate before we move on.

DOUG FORD'S GAS PLANTS

In 2018, I was organizing climate action among farmers and rural people. While leading kitchen table meetings and workshops with hundreds of farmers, I repeatedly showed a slide regarding current trends in greenhouse gas emissions for Canada:

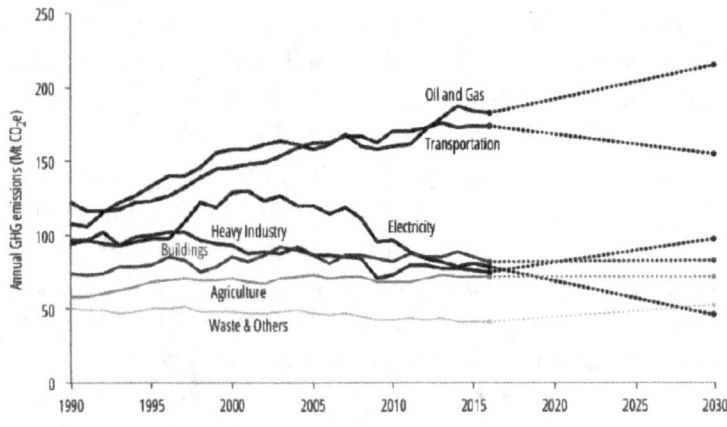

Of course, the oil and gas industry was the biggest emitter of greenhouse gases. However, most industries were increasing or maintaining their emissions at the time.

By far, the most promising trend in Canada was the falling emissions of the electricity-generating sector. That improvement was due almost entirely to the recent shutdown of coal-fired electrical generation in Ontario (after a long campaign by the Ontario Clean Air Alliance).

Then, at the end of 2018, Doug Ford was elected premier. His brother, former Toronto mayor Rob Ford, had achieved global notoriety due to his sexism, racism, and a series of drug-and-alcohol-related scandals. Eventually, a video was released showing the mayor smoking crack cocaine while commenting on political issues.

Rob Ford was the more notorious of the brothers. But when he died of cancer, his brother Doug stepped into his shoes, eventually becoming the leader of Ontario's conservative party and premier of the province. Doug Ford was part of a wave of "populist" right-wing leaders who were elected at the time, reminiscent of Trump but lacking charisma.

Once elected, Doug Ford promptly canceled nearly a quarter-billion dollars' worth of renewable energy projects across the province. This was based on ideological opposition to green energy—many people in conservative rural election ridings had been opposed to new wind turbines being built in their areas, and Ford saw this as an easy way to play to his base.

Unfortunately, this led to a sharp reversal of the previous emissions improvements for electricity generation, and subsequent conservative political appointments further consolidated the rollback.

Doug Ford put a climate-change denier in charge of the Independent Electricity Systems Operator (IESO). Despite the name, the IESO is not politically independent; it is a crown corporation responsible for predicting demand and managing provincial electrical systems.

Ford's politically motivated attacks on renewable energy—and his tendency to appoint political cronies instead of skilled civil servants—meant that by 2023, the IESO was publicly predicting shortages of electricity generation. They were also desperate to bring new generating capacity online, particularly to buffer the daily peaks and valleys of electricity demand.

The cheapest approach would have been renewable energy combined with "demand management" to reduce peak electricity consumption. This would have taken years to implement, and the IESO claimed that this made renewable energy impractical. Of course, it was *their* failure to plan and predict—their squandering of precious years of action during a climate emergency—that led to the so-called crisis.

There was another reason that the ruling conservative party didn't like renewable energy. The previous government had created programs to encourage communities and individuals to invest in renewable energy by promising to pay people who installed solar panels (for example) a guaranteed payment per kilowatt-hour over the years ahead. For all their imperfections, these programs successfully supported the growth of local renewable energy installation companies. And the money from the funding went to local communities (albeit mostly middle-class households who could afford the initial investment).

Doug Ford's conservatives didn't want to just *give* money to regular people for helping to solve a problem. Their *modus operandi* was to transfer money to their corporate donors and industry pals on a much larger scale.

The provincial government's proposal to address the promised energy shortage was to build a series of massive methane gas-generating plants at critical points across Ontario.

This would have cost billions of dollars and would have been a massive waste of public money. Federal regulations require most gas plants in Canada to shut down in 2035, including new capacity. This means that starting construction of new plants in 2025, after less than a decade of operation, was simply not cost-effective for private industry. (Indeed, renewables were already all-around cheaper to build than fossil generation.)

To sweeten the offer, the IESO offered a contract that would pay fossil fuel companies for these plants even after they shut down—in essence, giving billions of taxpayers' dollars to massive corporations for doing nothing.[194]

To counter public opposition, the IESO claimed that it was treating fossil gas as a "transitional fuel" on its way to a green future. Of course, the notion of methane as a transitional fuel was deeply phony. The IESO had been moving in the opposite direction since Ford's election.

According to the IESO's own figures, their new generating capacity was heavily dominated by gas and oil.[195] They had more than doubled their use of fossil fuels for electrical generation since 2017. While wind and solar generation had grown over five years, fossil fuels were being added at more than twice the rate of renewables.

Moreover, research had found that the negative impact of climate gas (because of fracking and leaks) was almost as high as coal—which gas was supposed to replace.

To add yet another source of outrage, analyses by the Royal Bank of Canada and the Ontario Clean Air Alliance showed that new natural gas plants were unnecessary and a combination of renewable energy and demand management would be sufficient. If the Royal Bank of Canada—the world's largest financier of fossil fuels—says that you don't need more gas plants, you know it must be true.

These plants would have been almost impossible to stop if it weren't for one unintended loophole.

When Doug Ford was elected, he wanted to make it easier for conservative municipalities to stop future wind farms. As a result, he put in place a policy requiring local approval for new projects.

Taking advantage of that loophole was our only hope of stopping the new gas plants without a long, uncertain, difficult struggle. We wanted to avoid the kind of prolonged grind that had failed to stop Line 9.

We found ourselves organizing against the provincial government at the municipal and local levels—the kind of grassroots organizing where a handful of dedicated people can truly make a big difference and where long relationships matter.

Organizations like the Ontario Clean Air Alliance, Environmental Defence, and the Canadian Association of Physicians for the Environment (CAPE) led efforts to block the gas plants at the municipal level. The advocacy of healthcare professionals like Dr. Mili Roy, Ontario chair of CAPE, was crucial since the new gas plants would significantly increase air pollution in the areas where they were built.

In mid-2023, the coalition won its first two victories, securing municipal resolutions against gas plants in both Toronto and Thorold.

The victory in Toronto wasn't a huge surprise. There was a strong environmental tradition against gas plants in the Greater Toronto Area. Indeed, a gas plant proposed for Toronto a decade earlier had been canceled in the face of public outcry and local organizing. (The cost to cancel the plant partway through development would grow to more than a billion dollars, which would contribute to the eventual defeat of the previous Liberal government.) That plant was eventually built near Napanee, Ontario (a short distance west of me).

The victory in Thorold was a coup, though. Thorold is a relatively small and rural municipality, and the province wanted to build a particularly large plant there.

Local organizers, the Ontario Clean Air Alliance, and Environmental Defence ran ads, called councillors, and mobilized their neighbors against the proposed gas plant. Their arguments—based on climate, public health, and fiscal prudence—prevailed. Thorold City Council voted unanimously against the proposed plant on September 19, 2023.

Though surely stung by this public rebuke, the IESO continued to try to get municipal support for new projects. One approach they used was requesting municipalities sign off on "blanket approval" for new energy projects, regardless of environmental impacts or public health and safety.

They did that next by coming to my region. In October, they put a resolution before Kingston city council to request blanket approval for new energy projects. City staff—including the climate manager—endorsed this proposal because they didn't understand the provincial context, or they didn't care.

This draft resolution was made public only a few days before the council meeting at which it was to be voted on—so we had to act fast.

Fortunately, we had strong climate justice networks to rely on. I drafted a community letter, which more than thirty prominent individuals and groups quickly signed on to.

We sent the letter and spoke to individual councillors. On October 17, I attended the council meeting to speak on behalf of the signatories.

The result? Success. Deputy Mayor Wendy Stephen moved an amendment to exclude fossil fuels from any endorsement.

The IESO wasn't done, of course. Less than a month later, I was tipped off that they had approached Loyalist Township, a small rural municipality immediately west of Kingston, with another request for blanket approval.

That municipality already had one small fossil gas generator, and the IESO hoped they would allow another.

We had very little time. In fact, by the time the proposed resolution became public (again endorsed by municipal staff), the deadline to request a formal delegation spot had already passed.

Tight on time, I updated our community letter from Kingston and relied on my connections with rural environmentalists and farmers to mobilize people in the municipality.

Over fifty people and groups—students, seniors, farmers, Indigenous people, professors, and concerned citizens—signed the community letter against the gas plant this time.

We encouraged people to call their councillors, write letters, and show up in council chambers on the night of the vote.

The community response was powerful, and the results decisive. Loyalist Township Councillors voted unanimously against the proposal. (In fact, a couple of councillors thanked me afterward, saying it was the biggest community engagement on any topic in their entire term.)

Two proposed gas plants remained: one slated for Napanee, the other for Halton Hills.

Everyone in the coalition knew Napanee would be difficult to win. Greater Napanee already had more than one fossil gas plant in the region and had been offered $4.8 million in provincial funding to accept an additional plant.

Many of us, including Environmental Defence, the Canadian Association of Physicians for the Environment, and the Ontario Clean Air Alliance, made delegations before the Greater Napanee Council against the proposed plant.

So many people wanted to speak against the plant that an entire council meeting was spent hearing those delegations, and the final decision had to be made at a subsequent meeting.

Despite our best efforts, the Greater Napanee Council approved a dramatically expanded gas plant.

I was at that meeting. There was no discussion or debate before the vote. In fact, the Napanee Council had a longer and more meaningful discussion about a single drainage ditch than about a fossil fuel project that would harm the future of the entire planet.

When asked for comment by the press, I said, in part:

> Greater Napanee was offered $4.8 million dollars as an "incentive" to expand a polluting gas plant. From the outside, it certainly looks like that money induced Napanee Council to rubber-stamp this project. The irony, of course, is that those millions are public dollars in the first place. Fossil fuel companies are bribing local communities with taxpayer money. Why should we be bribed with our own money?
>
> Federal regulations will require most gas plants to close by 2035 because of the air pollution they release. Building new gas plants is no longer financially viable—renewables are cheaper now—so Ontario's provincial government has offered to keep paying fossil fuel companies even after these gas plants shut down.
>
> That means more than a billion dollars of public money will be given to fossil fuel companies for doing nothing all at.
>
> Compared to that, a few million is pocket change. If Napanee Council was bought off by this proposal, they were bought off cheap.[196]

That multi-million dollar incentive was a key factor in the outcome. So was the striking lack of critical thinking and due diligence by councillors.

That the most prominent opposition to the plant came from Toronto-based organizations was also a factor. As in many places, there is an urban-rural cultural divide in Ontario. People outside of Toronto and the few big cities are often resentful of the fact that so many decisions are made in Toronto without consulting people in the rest of the province. Many rural people view those from Toronto as out-of-touch elites.

I'm sure that one of the reasons that councillors in Greater Napanee ignored opposition to the gas plant was because they thought the people opposed to it were not their constituents and would simply go away after the vote.

Another key problem was the coalition's failure to engage with the Mohawks at Tyendinaga. I believed—and continue to believe—that the Mohawks are the most able to organize and effect community opposition to ecocide in the region around Tyendinaga, thanks in part to their willingness to use direct action.

The good news is that the same coalition was successful in stopping the final proposed gas plant in Halton Hills. That municipality was more safely in the coalition's "home turf," and consisted of councillors more aware of the dangers of fossil fuels and more willing to listen to a variety of voices.

In the end, we stopped all but one of the gas plants. This is a pretty good batting average. Had all members of the coalition understood the factors needed for environmental wins in a rural area like Napanee, we could have won there, too.

But why, you might ask, would I include this story in a chapter about phantom victories?

It was, after all, a major win. Following our success in Loyalist Township, I gave interviews to national media. We stopped the emission of tens of millions of tonnes of greenhouse gases. We kept billions of dollars of public money from being funneled into the pockets of fossil fuel corporations.

The impact was dramatic. But what of the record? There are a few digital news articles and the digital minutes of a few small municipalities. A generation from now, what—if any—of that record might remain?

Will this success become yet another phantom victory? Our

very success, often on a short timeline, means that there are few records for public memory.

We won, and we need to make sure that people in the future can apply its lessons because that same path can lead to our future successes.

Cherish your victories, my friends. Celebrate them. Retell them. Embed them in print, art, and song. Make them last.

We need them very much.

TEN

The Richmond Dump

NAPANEE, ONTARIO
1988–PRESENT

Thanks to persistence, diverse skills, and an alliance between settlers and Indigenous peoples, a small group of organizers in Ontario defeated the largest garbage company in the world.

Waste Management is the largest garbage corporation in the world, raking in $15 billion annually from over 300 landfills.[197] With hordes of well-paid lawyers and lobbyists, the massive corporation is used to getting its way. When it can't use PR to bamboozle local municipalities, it can use deceptive "experts" and heaps of paperwork to overwhelm opposition at local planning boards or environmental review bodies.

At least, that's how it usually happens. However, in the case of the Richmond Dump, located near the Bay of Quinte in Eastern Ontario, things did not play out the way Waste Management intended. Waste Management pushed for a huge expansion of a local landfill. Instead, Waste Management was defeated by a small group of committed community advocates over a decades-long struggle.

If we want to understand how they won, we must know a few key things about the area's history, which was shaped by Indigenous struggles.

During the American Revolution, the British Empire allied itself with specific Indigenous groups to try to retain the territory it had occupied in the Americas. (This must have been a difficult decision for Indigenous groups, who were not well treated by either the British or the American colonists.) The Mohawks mostly fought with the British, but their homeland was mostly in what is now known as upstate New York. When the colonists won the Revolutionary War, the British granted their Mohawk allies land further north. In 1793, the British created a reserve called Tyendinaga on 375 square kilometers of land.

This area just north of Lake Ontario was also the destination of white settlers loyal to the British Crown who fled the newly independent United States. In the century that followed, many United Empire Loyalists and European immigrants settled in the area.* Bit by bit, those settlers took most of the land that had been granted to the Mohawks.

By the 1950s, the settler population of Richmond Township (adjacent to Tyendinaga) had become quite dense. New kinds of garbage—such as plastics—had become a problem.

In 1954, a British immigrant named Fred Sutcliffe launched a service to collect garbage from the settlement, which he would dump and burn on his farm. Local accounts from the time suggest that Sutcliffe was well-liked, if not responsible with environmental safety. Over the years, he expanded his operation, and new waste-handling regulations came into effect. In 1971, Sutcliffe received a Certificate of Approval for a nine-acre landfill accepting 15,000 tonnes of garbage per year.

In the 1980s, however, Sutcliffe did things that raised alarm in the community. He applied for a significant expansion of his landfill (see Figure 10-1). Few neighbors objected, but after the paperwork

---

* United Empire Loyalists were colonists loyal to the British Crown who relocated to what is now Canada, during and after the American Revolutionary War.

had gone through, Sutcliffe sold his business to an outside company called Tricil Ltd. His neighbors were outraged by the deception.[198] (Some believe Tricil quietly orchestrated the expansion to exploit Sutcliffe's good relationship with the community.)

GETTING ORGANIZED

Organized resistance to the dump expansion began immediately. In 1988, the Richmond/Tyendinaga Environmental Association formed and worked through official channels to try to limit the expansion of the dump. The process dragged on for years. While it did, the Richmond Dump was purchased by another company, which would eventually become Waste Management.

Meanwhile, in neighboring Tyendinaga, Indigenous people were using official channels to address even greater historical injustices. In 1995, Tyendinaga's Band Council filed a land claim for the Culbertson Tract, a large parcel of land illegally taken from the reserve in the 1800s. The tract is located between the existing reserve and the Richmond Dump. The Band Council would spend years negotiating in good faith for the return of that land while Canadian officials evaded and equivocated.

Dan Doreen, a member of the Mohawk Warrior Society at Tyendinaga, told me: "I don't think standing on the side of the road with a picket sign works for Indigenous people. It never has and never will. It's been 500 years of destruction."

In any case, the movement against the Richmond Dump continued through the 1990s. Thanks to organizers' tireless community education, it became more widely understood that the Richmond Dump site was an exceedingly terrible place for a landfill. The site's underlying geology consists of cracked limestone, a type of bedrock full of underground fissures and passages that can channel water quickly over long distances and in unpredictable directions. Once the groundwater in such limestone is compromised, the contamination is impossible to contain and can affect people living near and far.

The existing landfill had already compromised water quality in nearby wells, and life in a wetland and creek was dying.[199] Neighbors reported worsening infestations of rats.[200] Some residents started buying bottled water instead of drinking well water.[201]

Because of these clear ecological harms, residents were shocked when, in 1998, Waste Management announced a plan for a massive expansion of the Richmond Dump (see Figure 10-1). Waste Management planned to use the dump not only for garbage from the local area but also to truck in garbage from distant cities.

FIGURE 10-1

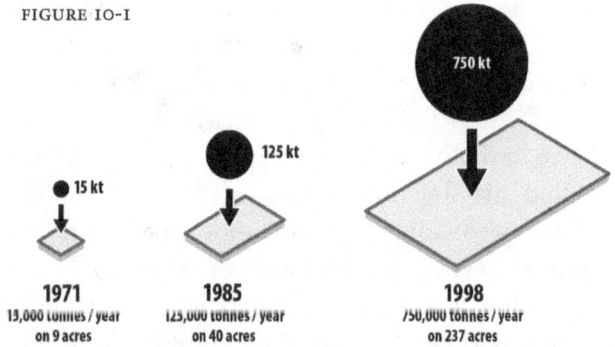

1971	1985	1998
13,000 tonnes / year	125,000 tonnes / year	750,000 tonnes / year
on 9 acres	on 40 acres	on 237 acres

Community members were horrified. They formed new anti-dumping groups (including the Concerned Citizens Committee of Tyendinaga and Environs, CCCTE) and organized community meetings against the dump. At one meeting, Mohawk Elder Andrew Maracle gave a vigorous speech against the dump and then collapsed and died.

However, the community persisted, and CCCTE retained environmental lawyer Richard Lindgren from the Canadian Environmental Law Association. With Lindgren's help, CCCTE began a series of legal challenges and public interventions to stop the dump expansion. This went on for more than eight years.

ESCALATION

Frustrated with a decade of glacial progress through official channels, anti-dump organizers escalated. In September of 2000, they organized a protest at which a petition was delivered to Waste Management. The protest became more militant, with the crowd repeatedly shouting down a Waste Management representative. Processions of marchers, cars, and tractors blocked traffic.[202]

CCCTE also created a petition against dump expansion, which, by 2005, had been signed by about 90 percent of area residents, thanks in part to door-to-door canvassing and regular protests.[203]

The campaign was also strengthened by support from the Mohawk community and Band Council Chief Don Maracle. In her fantastic history of the struggle, *Fighting Dirty: How a Small Community Took on Big Trash*, Dr. Poh-Gek Forkert writes: "I remember a public meeting at the Selby Community Hall in 2005 when Chief Maracle said that the Mohawks would never allow anyone to 'poison the people in their nation.' Frustrated, he warned, 'So, as part of your risk assessment, you better take into account civil unrest.' He paused to let the point sink in."[204]

This was not an idle threat. Militant action at Tyendinaga was on the rise. The community understood the importance of clean drinking water; Tyendinaga—and over a hundred other Indigenous communities—had been under a boil water advisory for years.

The government wanted to redirect community anger over the dump into a series of highly technical "consultations" that were implicitly meant to leave the problem to the experts. Forkert writes: "Tactic number one for the developer seemed to be to drown the opposition in paper and bafflegab. Residents attending the meetings were overwhelmed by the presentations especially with the details and data."[205] However, the community refused to be diverted.

Finally, in November 2006, the combination of legal action, education, and protest with the threat of direct action achieved an important win: the provincial minister of environment announced the expansion had been rejected.

It was an exciting and important victory. However, while *expansion* had been stalled, the Richmond Dump was still accepting garbage. The land and water were still being harmed; groundwater plumes of pollution and leachate were still poisoning wells and destroying nearby aquatic ecosystems. The damage continued.

Residents wanted the dump closed entirely, but government officials ignored them.

Government stalling was nothing new to the Mohawks at Tyendinaga. Official negotiation over the Culbertson Tract land claim dragged on. There, too, the damage continued. There was an active gravel quarry on the tract, grinding up the land and shipping it away at a rate of more than 800 dump truck loads per month.[206] The land the Mohawks were trying to reclaim was being dug up, ground into gravel, and shipped away.

In 2007—some twelve years into their land claim process—a group of militant Mohawks decided that they'd had enough.

THE MOHAWKS AND THE QUARRY

Members of the militant Mohawk Warrior Society occupied and shut down the quarry on the Culbertson Tract. Shortly after, they targeted a major rail line in Ontario—which crosses the reserve—blocking all trains for thirty hours. In that time, they stopped the movement of a truly impressive $100 million worth of freight.[207]

Next, they organized a National Day of Action on Indigenous

issues which included blockading the 401, one of the busiest high-ways in the world. These actions made for major news stories and led to some arrests, but police and government were unable to quash the militant actions.

The Mohawk warriors persisted despite repression partly because of their profound commitment. Mohawk Warrior Dan Doreen told me: "When I go out, we think things through. We think things through seriously." He explained: "You have got to be willing to give up your life. . . . That's what cops are most afraid of. When they look you in the eye and see that you are willing to die, they get scared of that. That frightens them."

Local governments were uncomfortable with the Mohawks' militancy. The township council called the warriors "malcontents" in contrast with the "legitimate Mohawk Government."[208] The head of the township council at the time was Margaret Walsh, who had been active in the anti-dump fight since the 1980s.

The official band council distanced itself from the militants; Chief Don Maracle said he supported the spirit of their actions but not their tactics.

It's not clear if he fundamentally disagreed but was trying to stake out a moderate position to take advantage of radical flanking by making the Band Council more appealing to the government by contrast, essentially saying *negotiate with us or you'll have to deal with them.*

In any case, Chief Maracle had been willing to promise that exactly those tactics could be used if the government did not shut down the Richmond Dump. Forkert remembers that "in a meeting at the Ministry of the Environment in Toronto, I watched him calmly but emphatically say, 'Not a single garbage truck will get through. If we have to shut the 401 down, we can do that again.' Ministry officials clearly heard the threat. There was a palpable silence in the room."[209]

While some of the settlers in the anti-dump movement were willing to condemn Mohawk militants as "malcontents," that militancy was critical for the anti-dump campaign's eventual success. The government constantly tried to channel community outrage into technical consultations and manageable procedures. However, a strong showing by the Mohawks Warrior Society helped ensure that didn't happen.

Forkert writes: "I can recall meetings when Mohawk warriors came with their flags depicting the silhouette of a warrior in profile with a golden sun behind on a red background. The men first circled the room and then went to the back to stand, arms crossed, silent, and just a little menacing. The warriors never did or said anything [at these meetings], but they were a presence."[210]

This multi-pronged approach worked. The citizen's group, mostly polite and law-abiding, worked its way through proper governmental channels and environmental assessments. Often, this is not enough—governments and corporations can overwhelm well-behaved community groups with nonsense, outlast them, or ignore them.

In this case, however, the Mohawk warriors were willing to bypass the theatre of phony consultation and use disruption and direct action. The government knew that if they defied community wishes during the campaign, the Mohawks could take action that would be unmanageable, messy, and expensive for those in power.

With continued community pressure and a legal challenge under the Environmental Bill of Rights, the Ontario Environmental Commissioner called for the Richmond Landfill to be closed in 2009. In 2011, it finally happened. The Richmond Landfill—which had been operating since Sutcliffe started collecting garbage more than fifty years earlier—was decommissioned.

Waste Management was unhappy; one of their officials "complained bitterly about being beaten 'by a bunch of poor farmers and an old Indian chief.'"[211]

Aspects of the struggle continue. Residents work for better monitoring of the leachate plume as they fight against Waste Management's attempt to restart a new landfill next door. However, opponents of the dump can claim their long campaign as a victory.

So how did they do it? How did they win?

VICTORY FACTORS

The community victory over the Richmond Dump was hardly a foregone conclusion. Around the same time, Waste Management pushed two other dump expansions in Ontario. "Citizen's groups in both places vigorously opposed the expansions," notes Forkert, "but failed to stop them."[212] What factors helped this struggle to win?

Tangible issues. The threat posed by the Richmond Dump was immediate and tangible. *We can't drink our water. There are rats, terrible smells, and dead wildlife.* Distant or abstract issues are difficult for organizers. The more imminent a threat, the easier it is to mobilize people. This imminence helped to catalyze early resistance by farmers and Indigenous people, both groups that can have a special attachment to—and feel a responsibility to protect—the land.

Strategic capacity. The groups opposing the campaign were able to develop *strategic capacity*; they included people from various backgrounds and with diverse skill sets. They could also work with outside experts, like Richard Lindgren, who understood the importance of community struggle. Legal and technical aspects are essential in these campaigns, but it's also important not to devalue other skills. If the fight becomes only a conflict of paid expert versus paid expert, the better-funded corporate side is likely to win. Outside experts must be able to work with community groups to support diverse tactics.

Building a community of resistance, persistence, and decreasing naiveté. This was a long campaign. People stayed involved because of the imminent threat but also because of long-term friendships with other organizers. ("You couldn't let people down.[213]")

Many of the settler organizers interviewed by Poh-Gek Forkert mention their growing political awareness. In the beginning, Mary Lynne Sammon said: "The whole thing was an eye-opener for me. We were babes in the woods. There was an innocence there."[214]

This disillusionment began as early as 1988, when, Forkert explained: "They now realized that they could not depend on their government to protect them. Had they been naive to think otherwise?"[215] By the end, Jeff Whan told Forkert: "I have come to understand that we cannot count on the Ontario government to protect the environment.[216]" Instead, Whan realized, the Ministry of Environment "sees their job as facilitating industry."[217]

Their growing awareness—and understanding that "business as usual" would not resolve the problem—turned them into a community of resistance willing to confront and challenge wrongdoing.

Organizational capacity. The community group developed a strong capacity (discussed below) for fundraising and communications, as well as intelligence. This capacity allowed them to mobilize their neighbors and sustain a long and often expensive struggle.

Alliance with Mohawks. It's unlikely the campaign would have succeeded without strengthened connections between settlers and Indigenous peoples. Forkert notes: "The alliance between the Mohawk community and the white population—the two groups had lived as two solitudes for centuries—was a critical development."[218] Lawyer Richard Lindgren said, "We would have had no chance without the involvement and co-operation of the Mohawks of the Bay of Quinte. That's the only reason we were successful during the first environmental assessment process."[219]

That alliance brought a new tactical repertoire to the struggle.

Diverse tactics and deterrence. The citizen's group became more militant over time. But they did not have to use very much direct action thanks to the threat of more successful direct action at Tyendinaga. Mohawk militancy was a powerful form of deterrence that forced the government to take the environmental assessment process seriously.

In *Full Spectrum Resistance*, I argue that successful movements typically need both moderates and militants and that those groups often benefit each other whether they are consciously cooperating or not.

Disruptive and direct action is a way of building power, explains Mohawk Warrior Dan Doreen. When advocating for change, he says: "Our leaders should go in with a position of power instead of a position of pity." He also recognizes that the division between official band councils and the grassroots Warrior Society is a form of divide-and-conquer by the federal government. "If we worked together, then we could have a lot more."

In the struggle against the Richmond Dump, anti-landfill organizers benefited greatly from the threat of Mohawk militancy. The ongoing possibility of direct action by Mohawks—which would be very disruptive and expensive for the Canadian economy—was a feature that shaped the government's response to the campaign.

Simultaneously with the Richmond Dump struggle, another group of organizers in central Ontario were trying to stop a new dump from being built at so-called Site 41. That struggle had likewise been focused on technical concerns and expert consultations for decades. Attempts to stop the landfill through official channels failed.

Once landfill construction began, however, a group of Indigenous women from nearby Beausoleil First Nation stepped in. The women used direct action, occupying the site and eventually mobilizing huge numbers of people who were able to stop the dump at Site 41.

In the case of the Richmond Dump, a sustained threat of Indigenous militancy pushed the government to shut down the project through "official channels." If there had been a similar looming threat against Site 41 during that consultation process, it's possible that the government would have canceled Site 41 early on to maintain an appearance of orderly government management and business as usual.

It's clear that in the Richmond Dump struggle, moderate landfill opponents benefited from nearby Mohawk militants. But it's less clear that Mohawks benefited from moderate activity.

For example, the citizens' group interrupted a Waste Management meeting at one point by standing up to sing "O Canada."[220] While I'm happy to see a rowdy crowd shut down PR nonsense, a show of patriotic nationalism is not a great way for settlers to endear themselves to Indigenous allies.[221]

And when Mohawk militants took over and shut down a quarry on their claimed land in 2007, some anti-dump advocates condemned them—even though that militancy would eventually be key to the success of the anti-dump struggle.

When talking about colonialism and privilege, we often talk about the unfair advantages that settlers have gained at the expense of Indigenous people, like access to land, better diets, and higher economic security.

But we don't usually talk about *this* kind of privilege: even when it comes to protest and resistance, Indigenous people often bear the brunt of the risks. At the same time, settlers may enjoy the results without endangering their safety and freedom through direct action.

So often, though, that *is* what happens. Indigenous people on the frontlines risk their safety and freedom by confronting fracking, oil pipelines, and other extractive industries. This resistance is for the common good, to protect us from a ghastly future of climate chaos.

It's long past time for more settlers to step up, step out of zones of comfortable privilege, and take on a level of risk that matches our privilege. That means taking more direct action in our campaigns, educating our fellow settlers about the importance of militancy, and helping to build models of resistance that allow Indigenous people and settlers to cooperate without forcing Indigenous people to shoulder most of the risk and hardship.

The Mohawks at Tyendinaga have seen some progress in their long struggle to reclaim land taken from them. In 2022, the Canadian government signed an agreement to transfer back 120 acres and a compensation package of $31 million to allow them to buy more land in the area.[222]

MOVEMENT CAPACITIES

In closing, let's take a moment to highlight how the anti-dump campaign developed some of its key resistance capacities. I'm particularly grateful to Dr. Poh-Gek Forkert for her exhaustive documentation of this struggle in *Fighting Dirty*. We owe her a debt for her detailed oral history interviews of organizers, some of whom have since passed.

Full Spectrum Resistance is organized into chapters based on the different capacities that movements need to succeed. Let's quickly glance at each of those in turn:

Recruitment and Training: The anti-dump campaign spent countless hours reaching out to friends and neighbors. Their success was reflected in the fact that about 90 percent of area residents signed a petition against the dump expansion, a truly impressive achievement.[223] Dr. Forkert writes: "The dump opponents set up a storefront office in Napanee—to dispense project information and collect signatures. Citizens opposed to the dump expansion walked the streets and shopping malls, went to church services, and knocked on doors. These efforts generated a record number of letters to the Ministry of Environment."[224]

Groups and Organization: The major anti-dump campaigns were organized by a handful of community groups, which usually consisted of perhaps a dozen core organizers and a broader network of supporters and volunteers. In the late 1990s to 2000s they benefited from collaboration with the Canadian Environmental Law Association (CELA).

Security and Safety: At its core, this campaign was about ensuring community safety: safe air, safe drinking water, and the long-term well-being of the land. This campaign didn't involve major risks to individual safety for people in the citizen's groups—that is, people didn't have to worry that corporate security goons would attack them. Their biggest safety risk was that the campaign would fail and that their community would be further poisoned.

Their Mohawk neighbors faced more significant safety and security risks because of their willingness to undertake direct action and because of structural racism and colonialism in general.

Communication: Some members of the citizens' groups brought their extensive communications experience to the movement. A retired software executive in the area, Jeff Whan, diligently developed a strategy by chairing a communications committee that met weekly and maintained a campaign website at leakyland.com.

Intelligence and Reconnaissance: Intelligence and research were critical for this campaign. As Forkert writes: "To be successful, every activist organization needs a secretary cum researcher cum historian to take notes at meetings and generate the minutes while providing context and background, someone dogged and meticulous and fueled by outrage. Someone to sort the paper trail, because it's certain that a big company's first strategy is to bombard outraged citizens with reports, studies, documents, and assurances from paid experts that all will be well. For the citizens who opposed the transformation of the Richmond Landfill into a mega-dump, Mary Lynne Sammon was that person for almost two decades."[225] (Sammon died of cancer in January 2015.)

The point of intelligence in resistance organizing isn't just to gather detailed files; we must also package and propagate that information in a way that makes people more able to take action. Forkert writes: "In the case of the Richmond Landfill, citizens needed to understand why the landfill should not be expanded at that side. Steve Medd, a resident and geologist, volunteered to educate the group about the physical characteristics of the site. In time, *almost everyone in the community knew* about fractured limestone, the thin glacial till overlaying the limestone plain, and why the geology of the site made it unsuitable for garbage disposal. Residents learned that leachate was produced by the action of rain and snowmelt on garbage piled on soil. They also learned about the high potential for leachate to contaminate wells and local streams, and the health effects of exposure to contaminated water and air."[226]

Counterintelligence and Repression: For the citizen's groups, this mostly involved dealing with corporate PR and attempts at deception. Of course, Mohawk militants (and other Indigenous resisters) have faced a full range of repressive tactics, from surveillance to lawsuits to arrests to threats of armed violence by the state and vigilantes.

Logistics and Fundraising: In part because of their strong recruitment and communications capacity, community fundraisers raised over $250,000 to pay for the anti-dump campaign, especially the costs of legal challenges.[227] (It's worth noting that until the 1990s, community groups could get "intervenor funding" to support their representation in environmental assessment hearings; Ontario Premier Mike Harris got rid of that.)

Actions and Tactics: It's difficult to summarize the many tactics used over decades as part of this campaign, which included protests and awareness-raising, legal challenges, and some direct action.

Community groups are most effective when they mobilize a large and diverse range of people and narrow their focus. As lawyer Richard Lindgren recounted: "Early on, I kept stressing to the citizens' group, 'Don't fight everything or you'll get burnout.' We focus on issues with the biggest bang for the buck."[228]

Organizers were hesitant to rock the boat at the beginning of the campaign, but came to understand the need for vigorous protest. Forkert spoke with Margaret Walsh, a long-time anti-dump activist who had served as reeve and municipal councillor: "I wondered whether her involvement with the dump issue ever hurt her at the polls. She had stood with placard-carrying protesters on the streets of Napance and several times—on her own dime, she hastens to add—went with delegations to Queen's Park [the provincial seat of government] to press their case against the landfill expansion. Such militancy is uncommon in Loyalist Napanee and environs. 'I never lost votes because of my involvement in the dump issue,' Margaret assured me. 'I probably gained a few.'"[229]

Campaigns and Strategy: The strategy of the campaign changed over the years. Part of the reason movement organizers were able to persist and adapt was because of their *strategic capacity*, including diversity and motivation. Forkert summarizes: "Although thousands of people in and around Napanee would get involved in some way (writing letters, baking cookies, selling raffle tickets, joining protests), the core group was made up of about a dozen people. That core would change over the course of years and decades, as members aged and passed away. Many were farmers or semi-retired farmers, but some brought a great deal of education and experience to the table—a geologist, an engineer, a software expert, a telecommunications expert, a teacher, an editor, a Mohawk chief with political smarts. They were a varied and creative bunch but formed a formidable alliance that got tighter as the years passed."[230]

Creative problem-solving was also key to their strategy, and one of their group's most creative strategic thinkers was the late Mary Lynne Sammon. Forkert quotes organizer Ian Munro: "The lasting memory I have of Mary Lynne was her amazing ability to think outside the box. Any time we had a meeting on any dump-related subject, she would offer options (always based on her broad-based knowledge) that often seemed to the rest of us to come out of thin air. More often than not, however, it turned out to be a novel and intriguing idea that made us all think about things differently. During the never-ending processes, our group followed a lot of different avenues. Many of those were thanks to Mary Lynne's unique contributions."[231]

Mike Bossio—an anti-dump activist who later became a Member of Provincial Parliament—shared with Forkert some similar memories about Mary Lynne Sammon. "She understood early on that this was going to be a long, drawn-out battle, and she was part of the core team because she had the perseverance necessary to get through the long spells where you just needed to grind away at data—and fundraising. Mary Lynne was so valued by so many because she was one of those unique individuals who came up with brilliant ideas, but more important was willing to put in the work necessary to execute those ideas."[232]

ELEVEN

Anti-Walmart Site Fights and Alt-Union Campaign

1990S–EARLY 2000S

Local communities and union groups challenge Walmart—the biggest company in the world—and win.

Winning a fight against the world's biggest company isn't easy, yet hundreds of communities in the United States and Canada managed to do just that in the 1990s and early 2000s. Not all those victories were permanent, but many have endured, and the cumulative impact of that resistance was huge.

Let's take a look at the "site fights" in which hundreds of community movements emerged in the 1990s and early 2000s to keep Walmart out of their towns.

Walmart was founded in Arkansas in 1962. It spread through the American South in part because it built its own vertically integrated distribution system. Much has been written about how Walmart's logistical edge allowed it to undercut other bargain chains and local businesses.

Cheap labor—particularly cheap women's labor—was another key to the corporation's expansion. Walmart's initial spread in Arkansas relied mainly on women in areas with high unemployment. Furthermore, Walmart's cheap goods were manufactured in Asia, again, by vast numbers of underpaid and poorly treated women.[233]

THE SITE FIGHTS

By the early 1990s, Walmart had saturated the American South with thousands of stores and began to expand into new territories—to the coasts and Canada.

This new round of expansion provoked resistance. Community groups worried that Walmart and other big-box stores would destroy local businesses and good jobs. Many were also concerned big-box stores would destroy walkable downtowns and cause automobile-friendly sprawl.

Al Norman's website, Sprawl-Busters.com, lists over 450 communities in the United States and Canada that organized opposition to Walmart and other big-box stores.

The techniques and tactics range from petitions and lobbying to lawsuits and direct action. Most anti-Walmart struggles have applied municipal zoning and bylaws to exclude big box stores.

In Greenfield, Massachusetts, organizers fought Walmart using grassroots tactics and direct democracy. When the town council rezoned land to permit a Walmart, Al Norman and others organized a campaign to stop it. "I didn't think we were going to win," Norman told me. There was no track record of success for anti-Walmart campaigns yet.

Norman and fellow campaigners plastered downtown Greenfield with signs reading "Stop the WAL" and "Shop Greenfield." They conducted a ballot initiative to reverse the zoning decision through municipal direct democracy. In 1993, the ballot initiative passed—barely—and kept Walmart out of town. Walmart tried again in the early 2000s, and Norman and other opponents were able to block the construction because the proposed site was on a wetland.

Many other towns followed a similar strategic template. Al Norman traveled across North America and the world speaking about the tactics and strategies used successfully in Greenfield and wrote multiple books about the topic, including *Slam-Dunking Wal-Mart.*

Most of the fights were in small communities, which used similar tactics focused on municipal planning and bylaws. Site fight tactics typically involved some combination of:

* ★ Lobbying municipal and local governments (and zoning and planning)
* ★ Petitions
* ★ Public awareness campaigns
* ★ Delaying and procedural tactics, including religious objections and environmental impact assessments
* ★ Lawsuits
* ★ Direct action.*

However, some site fights also occurred in major metropolitan areas. New York City and Los Angeles have largely managed to keep Walmart out of their cities thanks to fights supported by organized labor and alt-union OUR Walmart.[234]

COMMUNITY IMPACTS

Site-fight wins have had lasting benefits for the communities that fought them. The data we have now largely confirms the concerns of organizers in the 1990s.

---

* In perhaps the most dramatic example, direct actionists apparently hotwired two dump trucks on a Walmart construction site in Asheville, North Carolina, and used them to ram various structures, causing nearly a million dollars in damage.
http://www.citizen-times.com/cache/article/buncombe_news/60486.shtml
http://www.agrnews.org/issues/294/localnews.html

Research from Pennsylvania State University shows that US counties where a Walmart opened are now unequivocally poorer than counties that never had one.[235] This is partly because Walmart siphoned wealth from communities that would have otherwise recirculated among local businesses.

Despite Walmart's claims to provide employment, we now have conclusive data that Walmart eliminated jobs. For every poorly paid Walmart position a town gained, it lost an average of 1.4 other jobs.[236]

Furthermore, counties with new Walmarts had more crime than those without.[237] Even controlling for other factors, the cumulative effect was profound, according to the authors of one study: "Wal-Mart stores destroy civic capacity in the communities in which they locate by driving out local entrepreneurs and community leaders."[238]

That community damage would have a lasting impact. Walmart used a saturation model to expand, opening excess stores near its distribution centers to smother local businesses by beating them on both price and proximity.

However, once Walmart achieved this saturation, it still had more stores than consumer demand required. So, in the late 2000s, having wiped out local retailers, Walmart began shuttering less profitable stores in saturated areas.

This means that in some post-Walmart areas—especially in low-income, rural areas like parts of Appalachia—no local retail was left, even for essentials like groceries.[239]

By almost every metric, communities that had waged a successful site fight against Walmart ended up better off than if their site fight had failed.*

---

* Again, this is controlling for other factors like the community's initial affluence.

HOW DID THEY WIN?

What distinguished the successful site fights from the unsuccessful ones?

Recruitment was the critical capacity that allowed site fights to succeed; effective campaigns brought together a dedicated core group and mobilized supporters to do everything from signing petitions to protesting to attending city council meetings.

Al Norman of Sprawl-Busters highlights three common factors in group success: Grassroots engagement, solid organizing, and persistence.

Stacy Mitchell of the Institute for Local Self-Reliance suggests that the capacities needed are similar to other municipal campaigns and told me: "Women are often a key ingredient, too. It's not necessarily that they are female, but it's the activism of people who are taking a break from work (for kids) and thus have time and perhaps professional skills to bring to these campaigns."*

Stephen Halebsky also identified common factors for success in his book *Small Towns and Big Business: Challenging Wal-Mart Superstores*. Halebsky suggests that the biggest variable for success is "evidence of widespread opposition"—that is, the activists who won site fights were not only able to convince a lot of people, but they were able to *mobilize* those supporters to flood public meetings or sign open letters. (Halebsky also points to communications factors, like effective framing, use of the media, and publicizing corporate blunders.)

Movement building and recruiting opposition from diverse groups was also important, especially in urban areas. Historian Nelson Lichtenstein explains: "Wal-Mart was barred from these big blue cities because a coalition of unions, liberals, and environmen-

---

* This is an interesting reversal of Walmart's historical exploitation of women.

talists, including a large slice of those elected officials representing African American and Latino communities, said no."[240]

There was a little bit of direct action here and there during site fights. For example, it wasn't the main part of the meal; it was more spice than rice.

THE LEGACY OF SITE FIGHTS

Site fights didn't stop Walmart in its tracks. That's hard to do with a powerful corporation that is frequently backed by various levels of government.*

However, towns with a committed anti-Walmart movement had a high success rate; Al Norman lists nearly more than 450 such towns on his website, and that's only a partial listing. Using that data, political economist Dr. Joseph Baines looks at the peak of the site fights in 2008, when seventy stores were permanently or temporarily blocked.[241] Since each store has an estimated annual revenue of around $50 million, this represents an impact of $3.5 billion to the corporation in that year alone. That's an enormous number, and it doesn't consider the municipal subsidies that Walmart was deprived of or the escalating resources that Walmart had to put into lobbying and lawyers to try to suppress site fights.[242]

The financial crisis of 2008 was an opportunity for anti-Walmart organizers; victories that had been temporary or precarious became permanent as Walmart scaled back expansion plans.

These site fights also saved local jobs; the average Walmart store employed about 340 people at that time.[243] We know that each

---

* Nonprofit Good Jobs First points out that "Walmart has received over $1.2 billion in tax breaks, free land, infrastructure assistance, low-cost financing, and outright grants from state and local governments across the country". [Quoted in Mattera and Purinton 2004, in Carolina Bank Muñoz, *Building Power from Below*, 5.]

new Walmart job eliminated about 1.4 local business jobs, which means that site fights in 2008 saved over 33,000 local jobs.[244]

Since each site fight relied on a handful of organizers, that's an impressive impact per anti-Walmart activist.

I asked Norman what advice he would give to his former self. He said, "Be proactive. Don't wait for them to arrive."

"I've been telling people for twenty years," Norman explained. "You can stop Walmart with one sentence: No retail stores exceeding 50,000 square feet in commercial districts . . . If you want to spare yourself having the agony of a campaign, just change the zoning," he says.

Too often, he says, community activists get put on the *defensive* and are dragged into long, complex campaigns. Instead, communities should take the initiative and use "offensive zoning" to exclude bad practices in advance.

"Big corporations can be stopped," he says, "but the longer you wait, the harder it is."

THE ALT-UNION STRUGGLE BEGINS

While many of the site fights were successful, Walmart could still open thousands of new stores in North America and around the world.

So, as Walmart destroyed local businesses and jobs, the struggle against it shifted. Working conditions became the new battlefield.

Walmart's treatment of employees is notoriously bad. As discussed above, Walmart's profitable expansion would not have been possible without exploiting (primarily female) workers in its stores and manufacturing suppliers. It pays its workers so little—and gives them such unreliable hours—that a quarter of American Walmart workers say they don't have enough food to meet their basic needs, and Walmart workers are one of the biggest groups of food stamp users in the US.[245]

As it expanded, Walmart also gained a reputation for firing workers who became inconvenient: pregnant women, people with minor health conditions, and elderly employees who used the bathroom too much. And, of course, people who complained about the working conditions.

By the turn of the millennium, Walmart had become the largest corporation in the world, as measured by number of employees. And so unions—which had largely ignored Walmart during its early expansion—began to try to unionize those large numbers of mistreated workers.

Traditionally, unions employ tactics at one workplace at a time. (As a union organizer, I participated in many of these union drives across Canada.) The goal is to get as many workers as possible to sign confidential union cards, hopefully bringing unionization to a vote quickly enough that the employer can't respond effectively. It can be risky—anti-union employers can try to repress or fire pro-union employees (though this is often illegal). However, once they are at the negotiating table, unionized workers at a particular store or office can have a lot of leverage.

Walmart executives were so ruthless that if a union succeeded in forming at a given store, they would shut it down (as they did in Jonquière, Quebec, in 2005, among other places).²⁴⁶ Walmart's scorched-earth approach, their willingness to discard profitable stores to avoid giving workers even token wage increases, has made traditional unionization drives untenable.*

A new group called OUR Walmart stepped in to use new tactics and approaches.

---

* At the same time, Walmart was trying to rehabilitate its public image through "greenwashing"—buying solar power and putting in place superficial "sustainability" policies. By positioning itself as an "environmental leader," the company hoped to divide opponents against each other, pitting labour against environmental and community groups.

OUR WALMART

Founded in 2010 with support from the United Food and Commercial Workers (UFCW) union, OUR Walmart emerged from the corporation's quashing of previous union organizing efforts.

For one, OUR Walmart did not limit its organization to one store at a time. Instead, they worked to scale up and bring together workers from many stores nationwide. Their grassroots approach emphasized the needs and leadership of the workers, cultivating grassroots leaders at individual stores who could coalesce into larger regional or national campaigns.

OUR Walmart also used online tools for mobilization. By bringing together people from different stores online, workers could see that they weren't alone and that many workers across the country shared the same problems and desire for change.

Critically, OUR Walmart immediately translated the relationships built online into real-world action, and that action didn't look like traditional union organizing.

OUR Walmart used wildcat strikes and store blockades to show strength and disrupt particular Walmart stores, especially using coordinated action on big shopping days like Black Friday.

These short-term pickets and parking block blockades were easy to spread and imitate. Organizers also pursued bigger targets, like disrupting shareholder meetings. These actions were logistically straightforward but were also bold and, in some ways, risky for precarious workers.

An OUR Walmart strategist compared their approach to the Industrial Workers of the World, which in the early 1900s emphasized disruption and direct action over contracts and collective bargaining.

This approach helped build a grassroots movement of Walmart workers who understood their collective power and the power of collective action. As a result, more people joined the movement.

It also won some tangible victories from Walmart. A campaign called "Respect the Bump" won accommodations for pregnant workers. OUR Walmart also squeezed out a program to help move some precarious workers into full-time positions. And, perhaps most importantly, it won increases in the minimum wages starting in 2015.

Walmart—unable to simply shut down the affected stores—resorted to sneakier tactics. They hired military contractor Lockheed Martin to spy on union organizers.[247] They illegally fired workers.[248] One Walmart executive was caught trying to bribe an organizer to get a list of pro-union workers.

None of those repressive efforts were able to stop the campaign. However, in 2016, OUR Walmart faced its most significant setback: loss of funding.

OUR Walmart members were asked to pay $5 in monthly voluntary dues to sustain the campaign. However, most of the campaign's funding—millions of dollars per year—still came from the UFCW, which announced in 2016 that it would withdraw its funding.

It's disappointing, but perhaps not surprising, that traditional unions depend on dues-paying members, and a campaign like OUR Walmart—important and innovative as it was—didn't generate new UCFW members. The campaign is continuing, albeit with fewer resources.

UNION WINS IN CHILE

While organizing Walmart workers in North America has proved difficult, unions in one Latin American country have had a series of overlooked wins.

As part of its expansion into Chile in the early 2000s, Walmart bought a controlling interest in a Chilean retail chain, D&S.[249]

But as part of this deal, Walmart had to accept the existing unions, a story Carolina Bank Muñoz tells in her book *Building Power from Below*. Walmart tried to import its anti-union tactics to Chile—but militant and militantly democratic Chilean unions were able to fight back effectively.

Walmart tried to ban workers from talking about union business during their lunch breaks, even though "the ability to meet and discuss union business is considered a fundamental right in Chile."[250] Workers instead organized community meetings in front of Walmart stores, using a microphone and speakers to talk about their "miserable working conditions" to co-workers, customers, and community members. Whenever Walmart security unplugged their sound system, they plugged it in again. Walmart tried intimidating workers by videotaping meetings, writing down names, and having security guards loom over participants.[251]

But the workers did not stop. They were bold and persistent in the face of these intimidation tactics and had community support.

However, the Walmart unions in Chile don't have the same structural power as established unions in the United States or Canada. Indeed, during the right-wing military dictatorship of Augusto Pinochet, which lasted from 1973 to 1990, trade unions were banned.* While the right to strike and bargain collectively is part of labor relations law in many countries, the complex procedures involved require specialized bureaucracies of lawyers and experts from all sides—the employer, the union, and the government—often leaving rank-and-file workers out of ongoing decision-making.

However, Walmart workers in Chile need more paid staff and

---

* The dictatorship was, of course, the result of a CIA-backed coup against the democratically elected President Salvador Allende. Pinochet, with the backing of the United States, brutally suppressed unions and other social movements with a perpetual campaign of violence, torture, and murder targeting social activists.

more resources.[252] Regarding structural power, these Chilean unions have more in common with OUR Walmart than, for example, the Teamsters. As a result, these Chilean workers have had to use more innovative and creative tactics. Chilean union organizers have pursued a social movement organizing approach. Unable to depend on labor-relations bureaucracy, they have instead built their community power through a grassroots approach and participatory democracy, like the meetings discussed above.

For Professor Carolina Bank Muñoz, union power in Chile boils down to three key factors: Strategic capacity, union democracy, and militancy.[253] Bank Muñoz explains: "By militancy, I mean confrontational, disruptive, direct action tactics that workers and their organizations use to coerce employers to meet their demands," including "strikes, blockades, and sabotage."[254]

Retail workers in Walmart stores have disruptive power. As Bank Muñoz points out, that's especially true for skilled workers like butchers, bakers, and fishmongers, who are harder to replace.[255] Because retail workers' disruptive power is limited, Chilean unions use more immediate "flexible militancy." For example, suppose a Walmart manager is harassing a cashier for taking a bathroom break. In that case, the cashiers can immediately stage a slow-down, or butchers can refuse to cut meat in solidarity. Direct action can be used responsively day-to-day and hour-to-hour.[256]

The disruptive potential is far stronger for warehouse workers. Since Walmart has only three centralized warehouses in Chile, a warehouse workers' strike can immediately paralyze the whole distribution chain. A strike in 2006 helped to build union power for collective bargaining, and warehouse workers have been able to win "significant wage increases, vacation time, a union office, health and safety provisions, and more."[257] Walmart's tremendous logistical strength is also its weakness.

Not only were they able to retain their existing unions, but they were able to recruit new workers. The result is that most of Walmart's 38,000 workers in Chile are unionized.[258]

THE FOOTHOLD AND THE BEACHHEAD

Dedicated organizing, cross-demographic alliances, and diverse tactics were critical in places where Walmart was defeated. These strategic practices are often key to how movements win.

However, if we want to understand why Walmart won where it did (and why labor and community organizers won where they did), we need to understand one more idea: the *foothold*.

Military strategists would call this idea the *beachhead*.

Consider the site fights against Walmart. Virtually all the communities that defeated Walmart won because they kept Walmart from establishing a foothold. They created bylaws that would ban stores like Walmart. They prevented land from being rezoned for Walmart. They did everything possible to keep Walmart from establishing any presence in their communities.

Walmart understood this principle very well. They knew they could easily expand and drive out local businesses once they established one store in a town or a county. They also knew the local opposition would feel psychologically defeated and give up. (For example the city of Guelph, Ontario, gave heavy resistance to Walmart at first, but once the first store was built, a second Walmart met with almost no resistance.)

Once construction started at a Walmart store, they were unstoppable (despite occasional acts of sabotage). This is how it works for military beachheads as well. A military might spend vast amounts of effort gaining a beachhead—as the Allies did at Normandy late in WWII)—but expansion becomes cheaper and easier once they are established. The best way to defeat an invasion from the sea is to prevent a beachhead from being established—to meet the invaders with full force and drive them back into the sea, as the Athenians did at Marathon.

The idea of the foothold applies to labor organizing, as well. This is why Walmart responded dramatically to any efforts at unionization. They knew that if a single store were unionized, then potentially all their stores could be unionized. It was, therefore, more strategically advantageous for them to take drastic measures—like shutting down profitable stores—than to allow a union to establish a foothold within the corporation.

Contrast that with Chile, where labor has successfully contended with Walmart. Those wins have occurred because the union already had a foothold in the chains that Walmart purchased and could leverage that power.

Every effective movement must consider how winning even one foothold can make a difference. We should also remember how important early and decisive action is to prevent those in power from gaining footholds in their wars against us.

Patterns of Resistance

Writing *How Movements Win* has been a source of joy and optimism for me. Although I've been involved in movements since I was a teenager, while researching this book, I found new stories that will nourish and inspire me for years to come.

As a reader, I hope you have also found new reasons for optimism in these pages. I hope your spirits have been lifted and you can see new avenues for action.

Some stories in this book were surprising to me. However, despite the variety and diversity of these examples, I have repeatedly found the same patterns behind movements that win.

Writing this book has strengthened some of my core beliefs about how social movements make change—in particular, the need for direct action, coalitions across differences, and the importance of building movement capacity at the grassroots level.

I found twelve *key patterns* in these stories. For simplicity and coherence, I'll place these twelve patterns into three groups: *purpose*, *action*, and *organization*:

PURPOSE:
   1) A Tangible Common Goal
   2) Positive Vision

3) Urgency (Imminence/Emergency)
4) A Common Enemy

ACTION:
5) Initiative and Escalation
6) Disruption and Direct Action
7) A Common Tactic and Collective Action
8) Diversity of Tactics and Radical Flanking

ORGANIZATION:
9) Coalitions Across Difference
10) Movement Capacity
11) Participatory Decision-Making and Democracy
12) Persistence and Endurance

Let's begin with *purpose*. Our first four patterns all have to do with the goals and context of a movement. What do they want to achieve, and what environment are they operating in?

1) A TANGIBLE COMMON GOAL

In all these stories, community members and activists from different backgrounds had to rally together around *a tangible common goal.* They wanted to accomplish something specific and were able to do it together.

When Revolution of the Heart convened, its goal was clear: removing a specific colonial statue. That clarity and the ability to organize at a specific location were essential to its success.

Likewise, the struggle against the Richmond Dump was about a specific piece of land and community. There were particular people, wells, and wildlife being adversely affected by the dump. That made it easy to focus efforts on the problem's source and organize and unify community efforts.

The same was true for the campaigns around Parcel C, the Green Bans, the Wyhl Reactor Site, and many others.

All these groups could have chosen more abstract or diffuse goals. The Revolution of the Heart could have chosen to focus on "colonialism" in general, but that kind of vague, amorphous system is much harder to rally around.

Likewise, the Richmond Dump organizers could have focused on opposing the *concept* of waste in general—but would 90 percent of their neighbors have signed a petition against "waste"? It's very difficult to mobilize people to fight an abstraction.

I'm not saying we shouldn't oppose harmful systems or name them as things we want to change—to the contrary. However, if we're aiming to change big and abstract systems, we need to find intermediate goals and stepping stones that will let us achieve wins and build momentum.

2) POSITIVE VISION

While many of the stories in this book were oppositional, at least in part, successful movements were also guided by a *positive vision of what they wanted to create or protect.*

Parcel C organizers didn't just want to *stop* a parking garage; they wanted a community center for Boston Chinatown.

The radical unionists of the Green Bans wanted to protect specific neighborhoods and places. But they also wanted to forge an intersectional working-class movement in which unions also fought racism, homophobia, and imperialism. They wanted to build a "socialist world with a human face, an ecological heart, and an egalitarian body."

Many Indigenous-led movements discussed—like the Wet'su-wet'en struggle or the Revolution of the Heart—were about more than Indigenous survival; they were about reshaping the larger society to become more just and self-aware.

Indeed, sometimes the method of opposition *created* the positive model needed—like how the camp opposed to the Wyhl nuclear reactor created its own "college" and eventually became a nature reserve.

A clear, positive vision allows us to be more strategic and use our limited resources as community activists. It guides us, gives us a direction to move toward, and motivates and sustains organizers and supporters. Few people want to participate in a social movement if the only options are different kinds of defeat or if struggle only prolongs the inevitable.

People need a positive, transformative vision of a future worth living in. Now, especially.

3) URGENCY

Just because a problem exists doesn't mean people will act against it. Something needs to motivate people to get involved rather than wait for someone else to solve the problem. There must be some reason to set aside business as usual so that people go to the streets instead of staying home and watching Netflix.

Often, that reason is *urgency.* People respond much more actively to the threat of imminent harm than to something that *may* be a problem one day.

There's a reason activists have reframed climate change as a climate "emergency." Climate change is notoriously difficult to organize against because it can feel so nebulous and distant.

The environmental justice wins described in this book are tied to specific, tangible plans and specific, urgent threats. The Brent Spar was on the verge of being sunk. Doug Ford's gas plants were within weeks or days of being approved. The Richmond Dump was an active and growing threat to groundwater.

4) A COMMON ENEMY

Rallying people from different backgrounds around a joint campaign isn't easy. A tangible goal helps, and so does an emergency.

But one particular thing helps people put aside their differences: a common enemy.

In the struggles against the Northern Gateway and Line 9 pipelines, that common enemy was fossil fuel giant Enbridge. It's often a corporation, whether Unocal at Umbergaon, Waste Management at the Richmond Dump, or Walmart . . . everywhere.

Other times, the common enemy is the government: the German government in the struggle at Wyhl or the UK government in the case of the movement for nuclear disarmament.

Governments, though, can be sprawling. It's best to put pressure on specific figures and decision-makers whenever possible. Opponents of the Brent Spar painted Prime Minister John Major as a "redundant rig" to be dumped. Organizers of the 504 Disability Sit-ins focused much of their effort on Joseph Califano, the federal secretary of Health, Education, and Welfare.

That's the last pattern in the purpose and context group. Next, let's look at four more patterns: those of *action*.

5) INITIATIVE AND ESCALATION

In these stories (and in the wider world!), we see again and again that officials in corporations and government funnel dissent into bureaucratic or technical channels where community power can be controlled and dominated.

The United States government stalled the implementation of the disability rights measures in Section 504 of the Rehabilitation Act of 1973 by starting another review of regulations. Opponents of Line 9, the Richmond Dump, and the proposed nuclear waste dump spent years engaging in technical and bureaucratic reviews.

The City of Kingston tried to direct opposition to a colonial statue into a committee discussion about how the wording of a plaque might be adjusted.

Eventually, though, activists broke from those systems, *seized the initiative*, and went outside official challenges to do something bold and challenging. Activists kept their eyes on the prize, focusing on the specific tangible outcomes they wanted to achieve so they could avoid being derailed by a bureaucratic process that was meant to stifle them.

Sometimes this meant escalating the struggle, raising the stakes. Site occupations or sit-ins (like Revolution of the Heart, the Brent Spar, Wyhl reactor site, and the 504 disability sit-ins) were all meant to escalate the struggle and keep it from being ignored. They also created a sense of urgency that people could rally around to crystallize abstract issues into clear and tangible problems to be confronted.

Smart groups can also take the initiative by being proactive or preemptive. Al Norman's ultimate advice to stop corporations like Walmart was to put in place zoning bylaws that would explicitly pan big-box stores, avoiding the need for a site fight altogether. The struggle against the Energy East pipeline was likewise successful because of its willingness to preempt the bureaucratic hearing of the National Energy Boards with disruption and direct action.

6) DISRUPTION AND DIRECT ACTION

Disruption and direct action are among the most powerful tools we have as movement workers. In so many campaigns, our worst enemy is *business as usual*. Business as usual means the constant march of gentrification, corporatization, and growing inequality (as with the Green Bans, Parcel C, and the struggle against Walmart).

Business as usual also means the gradual accumulation of a

threat that could eventually become catastrophic, as with climate change or nuclear war.

Direct actions such as sit-ins, strikes, and blockades provide powerful tools to disrupt or stop business as usual.

Disrupting business as usual has many benefits. One is that it creates a strategic dilemma that those in power feel pressure to resolve. Recall how the Revolution of the Heart was able to get a quick response in part because city hall didn't know how to manage them or control such a bold action.

Direct action like the rail blockades of Shut Down Canada can create a strong economic cost that corporations and governments can't tolerate. The same was the case for the Brent Spar struggle, which combined both an occupation and boycotts to produce a high economic and political cost for those in power.

The bureaucratic management of dissent—through hearings or courts—is meant to put activists on a field of struggle that is rigged in favor of big corporations and colonial governments. It is meant to put us on a plane of conflict where we are at a disadvantage.

The benefits of direct action—and taking the initiative—are that *we* get to decide where conflict happens. We leverage the power of asymmetry. We choose a place where those in power are weak and *we* are strong. We get more control of the narrative.

7) A COMMON TACTIC AND COLLECTIVE ACTION

Movements that win use *collective action* of some kind. Individual actions alone—even good actions like buying fair trade coffee or flying less—cannot overturn entrenched systems of power.

The boycotts against Shell, marches of the nuclear-disarmament movement, and the construction bans in Sydney were all examples of common tactics that brought together people from many backgrounds to pursue a common cause.

But that's not the only way to do things. Indeed, collective action can be even more powerful when it involves many kinds of action at once.

8) DIVERSITY OF TACTICS AND RADICAL FLANKING

The most powerful movements use many tactics simultaneously—from petitions to legal challenges to direct action. This maximizes the impact by encouraging many different people to participate in the way that best suits them, using their particular gifts and skills at a risk level they feel comfortable with.

Sometimes, groups diversify their tactics because of the failure or shortcomings of a broader movement, as with the Committee of 100 and the Spies for Peace (and, to some extent, Energy East).

Ideally, a strategy of diverse tactics is intentional, as with the 504 disability sit-ins.

Smart use of diverse tactics can also strengthen a movement through radical flanking, as we saw in the struggles against the Richmond Dump and the nuclear waste dump in South Australia.

Radical flanking at work during Revolution of the Heart's effort to remove the statue of John A Macdonald. Kingston officials had ignored requests to take down the offensive statue for years. However, the escalation of direct action meant that a negotiated removal of the statue was suddenly the most appealing option, especially after the toppling and destruction of colonial statues in other cities.

9) COALITIONS ACROSS DIFFERENCE

To generate the political strength needed to create substantive change, movements that win create powerful coalitions across differences.

The Green Bans were not only a struggle to preserve green space but also for working-class neighborhoods and the rights of women, Indigenous People, and queer people.

Opponents of Doug Ford's gas plants were able to rally students and seniors, Indigenous people and farmers, climate justice advocates and public health experts. The struggle to salvage Parcel C for Chinatown likewise rallied not only the community but lawyers, healthcare advocates, and Quakers.

This ability to organize across differences is critical. Bridge-builders who convene supporters from diverse communities can, of course, increase the number of people and resources involved. However, they also bring together new perspectives that boost a movement's *strategic capacity*.

The organizers of the 504 disability sit-ins would not have succeeded without the *solidarity* they cultivated to bring together disability rights activists along with Black Panthers, unionists, queer organizers, and the United Farm Workers.

Such alliances can open new possibilities for transformative action and dramatically increase a campaign's overall capacity. Indeed, along with a diversity of tactics, cooperation between allied groups is essential to building healthy and strong ecologies of struggle.

10) MOVEMENT CAPACITY

Effective organizers *must* consider the specific capacities needed to reach their goals. Capacities like recruitment, communications, security, and logistics.

My book *Full Spectrum Resistance* was structured with a chapter for each of these important capacities, asking: "How do you recruit the people you need and keep them? How do you organize into groups that can cooperate and get things done? How do you moderate internal conflict? How do you reach out to new allies and supporters? How do you protect yourselves and your comrades from repression? How do you gather the intelligence you need to choose good targets? How do you work out the strategy and tactics you need to mobilize force in a rapidly changing political conflict? And how have movements of the past done these things?"

All movements need strategy and tactics. Movements must reach large numbers of people—like campaigns for Nuclear Disarmament—and more strongly develop their communications capacity. Groups that take on bigger risks—like the Spies for Peace or the Green Ban organizers—must build their skills in security and counterintelligence. And organizations that want to organize difficult or prolonged occupations—like those of the Brent Spar or the Wyhl Reactor Site—must master logistics if they want to win.

It's also important to look at building not just single campaigns, but enduring and intersectional *movements*. When we build successful movements, we can make transformative changes on a much larger and more lasting scale than any one campaign.

11) PARTICIPATORY DECISION-MAKING AND DEMOCRACY

Each victory described in this book involved democratic decision-making in how activists organized themselves and wanted society to function.

When I spoke to Hereditary Chief Na'Moks of the Wet'suwet'en, I asked him what he ultimately wanted to attain. "Democracy," he told me.

Remember the story of the Green Bans? When the suburban women in Hunter's Hill wanted help from the builder's union, the union agreed to help *on the condition* that the residents vote in favor of a green ban.

The campaign around Parcel C converged on a people's referendum and was meant to capture the collective wishes of Boston Chinatown.

The petition gathered by opponents to the Richmond Dump—boasting signatures from 90 percent of residents—showed the democratic will of the community.

Operating in a democratic and participatory way is a means of building strong movements and strategic capacity.

In contrast, some movements mentioned suffered greatly from a *lack* of democracy. The early anti-nuclear movement in the UK was stymied in part by the paternalistic approach of Canon Collins. The potential of the Green Bans was ultimately thwarted by the hierarchy of Gallagher and the national union.

12) PERSISTENCE AND ENDURANCE

Movements that win are movements that *last*. In his book *The Strategy of Social Protest*, William Gamson argues that social movements that can last until a broad societal crisis are likely to achieve their goals.

Movements need persistence for many reasons. One is that building relationships—building movements—takes a lot of time.

This book includes several examples of movements that won quickly. Revolution of the Heart reached its goal after only ten days of action, while some of our municipal campaigns against Ford's gas plants lasted less than a week.

But those efforts succeeded *because* they were the manifestation of many years of groundwork and relied on relationships and networks that had already been cultivated.

Building movements and making change isn't easy. There are times, though, when it's easier. A movement that can endure will eventually find opportunities that it can be ready to seize.

If the movement organizers are strategic, they'll have used that time to strengthen relationships, gather resources, and develop shared skills.

In other cases, movements don't need to *wait* for an opportunity so much as they need to *outlast* their opponent.

Many of the places protected by the Green Bans still exist today, in part because organizers were able to endure until the economic circumstances driving development had changed.

Even the win against Energy East resulted from delaying the process until that pipeline was no longer economically feasible.

I want to make an important caveat: Persistence is essential, but it doesn't win campaigns. If doing the same thing for six months doesn't lead to progress, doing the same thing over and over for six years is unlikely to be an improvement.

Endurance is valuable because of *what we do* with our time: grow our numbers, make alliances, learn new skills, try new tactics.

If we want to last in the long haul, however, we also need to think about how to retain people. What makes movement workers *want* to stick around? What makes them feel invested and have a stake in decision-making? How do we build a track record of wins that encourages people?

This quality, persistence, is in some way the result of all the other qualities combined. The ability to endure isn't just a matter of willpower—it's also a result of making many good strategic decisions along the way.

THE END OF THE BEGINNING

A nice, tidy novel can end in a nice, tidy way—resolve the major conflict, wrap up loose threads, and send the satisfied reader on their way.

This is not that kind of book. We do not live in a novel. The real world is messy, and there is much work to be done. There are many reasons movement workers are *un*satisfied.

So, let me conclude this book with a challenge: Let this not be the end. Help the stories, patterns, and victories in this book live beyond these pages.

If you haven't already, gather your friends and comrades to discuss and learn from the victories that inspire you. Don't just learn from the history of whatever movements you work in—learn from other struggles to cross-pollinate and invigorate your work.

Together, we can forge more intersectional and effective movements, building a better, more just, and more liveable future for all.

DISCUSSION QUESTIONS

QUESTIONS ABOUT SPECIFIC
CHAPTERS OR MOVEMENTS:

* What parts of this campaign or struggle do you find most memorable or inspiring?

* What aspects of this struggle did you find most surprising?

* What part of this story might you take back to your own work?

* What part do you wish more people knew about?

* Do any of the alliances or collaborations in this struggle feel relevant to your work or your area?

* Are the tactics in this campaign relevant to your work or your area?

* Are there specific people in this story you find yourself strongly agreeing with—or strongly opposed to?

* How did the groups in this chapter generate political force?

BIBLIOGRAPHY

"Afghanistan: It's About Oil." *Earth Island Journal*, https://www.earthisland.org/journal/index.php/magazine/entry/afghanistan_its_about_oil/. Accessed Sep. 16, 2024.

Akuno, Kali, et al., editors. *Jackson Rising Redux: Lessons on Building the Future in the Present*. PM, 2023.

Andre Henry. https://www.facebook.com/theandrehenry/posts/hope-is-the-fuel-of-revolution-the-problem-is-that-hope-is-that-hope-depends-on-/774764557801338/. Accessed Sep. 16, 2024.

"Another Network Is Possible." *Logic(s) Magazine*, https://logicmag.io/bodies/another-network-is-possible/. Accessed Sep. 15, 2024.

Baines, Joseph. "Wal-Mart's Power Trajectory: A Contribution to the Political Economy of the Firm." *Review of Capital as Power*, vol. 1, no. 1, 2014, pp. 79–109.

Bank Muñoz, Carolina. *Building Power from Below: Chilean Workers Take on Walmart*. ILR Press, an imprint of Cornell University Press, 2017.

Beaton, Cat, and Jim Green. *Standing Strong 2015–2017: How South Australians Won the Campaign against an International High-Level Nuclear Waste Dump*. No Dump Alliance, 2018, https://tinyurl.com/no-sa-dump.

Blum, William. *Killing Hope: US Military and CIA Interventions since World War II*. Updated edition., Bloomsbury Academic, 2022.

Boccaccio, Katherine. "Walmart Blocked from Entering New York City." *Chain Store Age*. Sep. 17, 2012, https://chainstoreage.com/store-spaces/walmart-blocked-entering-new-york-city.

Bose, Nandita. "Half of Walmart's Workforce Are Part-Time Workers: Labour Group." *Reuters*, May 25, 2018, https://www.reuters.com/article/business/half-of-walmarts-workforce-are-part-time-workers-labour-group-idUSKCN1IQ298/.

Brewood et al. *Beyond Counting Arses*. 1963.

Brooks, Keith. "What's Another $4 Billion amongst Friends?" *Environmental Defence*, Aug. 23, 2023, https://environmentaldefence.ca/2023/08/23/whats-another-4-billion-amongst-friends/.

brown, adrienne maree. *We Will Not Cancel Us: Breaking the Cycle of Harm.* AK Press, 2020.

"Buildup along Line 9 in Toronto without Emergency Plans Being Set." *CBC News*, Sept. 23, 2014, https://www.cbc.ca/news/canada/ toronto/buildup-along-line-9-in-toronto-without-emergency-plans-being-set-1.2774757.

Bulletin Of the Atomic Scientists. "Renewable Wackersdorf." In *Bulletin of the Atomic Scientists*, October 1989.

Burgmann, Meredith, and Verity Burgmann. *Green Bans, Red Union: Environmental Activism and the New South Wales Builders Labourers' Federation.* UNSW Press, 1998.

Burgmann, Verity. *Power and Protest: Movements for Change in Australian Society.* Allen & Unwin, 1993.

Cabral, Amílcar. *Revolution in Guinea: An African People's Struggle: Selected Texts.* Stage 1, 1974.

Carroll, Sam. "'Danger! Official Secret': the Spies for Peace: Discretion and Disclosure in the Committee of 100." *History Workshop Journal*, vol. 69, no. 1, Spring 2010, 158–176, https://doi.org/10.1093/hwj/dbp032.

Clifford, Stephanie. "Walmart Strains to Keep Aisles Stocked Fresh." *The New York Times*, 4 Apr. 2013, https://www.nytimes.com/2013/04/04/ business/walmart-strains-to-keep-grocery-aisles-stocked.html.

"CN Rail Layoffs Will 'Further Complicate' Tangled Supply Chain, Industries Say." *Global News*, Feb. 19, 2020, https://globalnews.ca/ news/6568323/cn-rail-layoffs-supply-chain-industries/.

Cone, Kitty. "Short History of the 504 Sit-in." *Disability Rights Education & Defense Fund.* Apr. 4, 2013, https://dredf.org/504-sit-in-20th-anniversary/short-history-of-the-504-sit-in/.

Cross, Roger, and Avon Hudson. *Beyond Belief: The British Bomb Tests; Australia's Veterans Speak Out.* Wakefield Press, 2005.

Dawson, Victoria. "Ed Roberts' Wheelchair Records a Story of Obstacles Overcome | Smithsonian." *Smithsonian Magazine*, March 13, 2015. https:// www.smithsonianmag.com/smithsonian-institution/ed-roberts-wheelchair-records-story-obstacles-overcome-180954531/.

Daschuk, James W. *Clearing the Plains: Disease, Politics of Starvation, and the Loss of Aboriginal Life.* University of Regina Press, 2013.

Duff, Peggy. *Left, Left, Left: A Personal Account of Six Protest Campaigns, 1945–65.* Allison and Busby, 1971.

"Emu Field." *Australian Nuclear and Uranium Sites*, Feb. 23, 2012, https://nuclear.australianmap.net/emu-field/.

Engels, Jens Ivo. "Gender Roles and German Anti-Nuclear Protest: The Women of Wyhl." *Le Demon Moderne : La Pollution Dans Les Sociétés Urbaines et Industrielles d'Europe*, edited by Christoph Bernhardt. Presses universitaires Blaise Pascal, 2002.

"Environmentalists Protest the Building of a Nuclear Power Plant in Wyhl" (1975). German History in Documents and Images (GHDI), https://ghdi.ghi-dc.org/sub_document.cfm?document_id=227. Accessed Sep. 11, 2024.

"Europe's Heatwave Is Forcing Nuclear Power Plants to Shut Down." *Quartz*, Aug. 6, 2018, https://qz.com/1348969/europes-heatwave-is-forcing-nuclear-power-plants-to-shut-down.

504 Sit-in 20th Anniversary | Disability Rights Education & Defense Fund. https://dredf.org/504-sit-in-20-anniversary/. Accessed June 27, 2024.

Forester, Brett, and Olivia Stefanovich. "Minister Signs Deal to Return Land to Tyendinaga Mohawk Territory." *CBC News*, Oct. 3, 2022, https://www.cbc.ca/news/indigenous/tyendinaga-culbertson-tract-claim-1.6604236.

Forkert, Poh-Gek. *Fighting Dirty: How a Small Community Took on Big Trash.* Between the Lines, 2017.

Goetz, Stephan and Hema Swaminathan. "Wal-Mart and County-Wide Poverty." *Social Science Quarterly* vol. 87, no. 2, 2006, 211–26. http://www.jstor.org/stable/42956120.

Government of Canada; Crown-Indigenous Relations and Northern Affairs Canada; "Statement of Apology to Former Students of Indian Residential Schools," September 15, 2010. https://www.rcaanc-cirnac.gc.ca/eng/1100100015644/1571589171655.

Graham, Caroline. "The Life and Times of Juanita Nielsen, 2007." *GreensMPs.* Mar. 24, 2023, https://web.archive.org/web/20230324085437/https://lee-rhiannon.greensmps.org.au/articles/caroline-graham-life-and-times-juanita-nielsen-2007.

Greenhouse, Steven, and Stephanie Clifford. "A Respite in Efforts by Wal-Mart in New York." *The New York Times*, Mar. 7, 2013, https://www.nytimes.com/2013/03/07/business/a-respite-in-efforts-by-wal-mart-in-new-york.html.

Guyon, Janet. "Why is the world's most profitable company turning itself inside out?" CNN Money, Aug. 4, 1997. https://money.cnn.com/magazines/fortune/fortune_archive/1997/08/04/229713/index.htm. Accessed Sep. 15, 2024.

Heilemann, John. "Why Wal-Mart Wants to Invade New York." *New York Magazine*, Aug. 5, 2005, https://nymag.com/nymetro/news/bizfinance/12399/.

"How Walmart Keeps an Eye on Its Massive Workforce." *Bloomberg.com*, http://www.bloomberg.com/features/2015-walmart-union-surveillance/. Accessed Sep. 15, 2024.

Indigenous Environmental Network. *Indigenous Resistance Against Carbon*. Aug. 19, 2021, https://www.ienearth.org/indigenous-resistance-against-carbon/.

"Labor Groups Are Taking On Walmart And McDonald's. But Who Will Fund Their Fight?" *HuffPost*, June 2, 2016, https://www.huffpost.com/entry/our-walmart-funding_n_574f4b70e4b0eb20fa0cac8b.

Lai, Zenobia, et al. "Lessons of the Parcel C Struggle: Reflections on Community Layering." *UCLA Asian Pacific American Law Journal*, vol. 6, no. 1, Spring 2000, pp. 1–43.

Lauby, Adrienne. "Transcript — Fading Scars: My Queer Disability History." *Pushing Limits*, Nov. 3, 2015, http://www.pushinglimits.i941.net/2015/11/03/transcript-fading-scars-my-queer-disability-history/.

Leong, Andrew. "The Struggle over Parcel C: How Boston's Chinatown Won a Victory in the Fight Against Institutional Expansion and Environmental Racism." *Amerasia Journal*, vol. 21, no. 3, Winter 1995/1996, pp. 99–119, https://doi.org/10.17953/amer.21.3.x223nj3686457318.

Lichtenstein, Nelson. "Wal-Mart Tries to Go to Town." *The American Prospect*, Apr. 19, 2011, https://prospect.org/api/content/6e453418-31ac-5f9b-b204-ee1abe8635a2/.

Malekar, Anosh. "Fish Wars in the Global South." *Medium*, Oct. 7, 2022, https://medium.com/@AnoshMalekar1968/fish-wars-in-the-global-south-465c9fe30d81.

The Man Behind the Pink Ban. https://web.archive.org/
web/20201201113557/https://grapeshotmq.com.au/2017/11/man-behind-
pink-ban/. Accessed Sep. 9, 2024.

"Maralinga Nuclear Tests 60 Years on: What Do We Know Now?" *NITV,*
https://www.sbs.com.au/nitv/the-point/article/maralinga-nuclear-tests-60-
years-on-what-do-we-know-now/ejjomsrlg. Accessed Sep. 16, 2024.

"Mass Occupation of Proposed Wyhl Nuclear Power Plant Site in
Germany, 1974–1977." Global Nonviolent Action Database. https://
nvdatabase.swarthmore.edu/content/mass-occupation-proposed-wyhl-
nuclear-power-plant-site-germany-1974-1977. Accessed Sep. 16, 2024.

Milder, Stephen. *Greening Democracy: The Anti-Nuclear Movement and
Political Environmentalism in West Germany and beyond, 1968–1983.*
Cambridge University Press, 2017.

Milder, Stephen. "The New Watch on the Rhine: Anti-Nuclear Protest in
Baden and Alsace." Arcadia 2013, no. 6, archived at *Environment & Society
Portal,* https://www.environmentandsociety.org/arcadia/new-watch-rhine-
anti-nuclear-protest-baden-and-alsace.

Miller, Ken. "Small-Town Budgets Hurting from Loss of Mini Walmarts."
Chicago Tribune, Jan. 20, 2018, https://apnews.com/general-news-88626a41
88414e7e8a5e8ffa189df210.

Mundey, Jack. *Green Bans and Beyond.* Angus & Robertson, 1981.

Neumark, David, et al. "The Effects of Wal-Mart on Local Labor
Markets." *Journal of Urban Economics,* vol. 63, no. 2, Mar. 2008, pp.
405–30, (cross-reference) https://doi.org/10.1016/j.jue.2007.07.004.

New Matilda. "The Green Bans That Saved Sydney." *New Matilda,* July 19,
2011, https://newmatilda.com/2011/07/19/green-bans-saved-sydney/.

New Statesman Magazine Subscription. https://web.archive.org/
web/20171221023119/https://subscribe.newstatesman.com/. Accessed Sep.
16, 2024.

"1970s: Victoria St Squats, Sydney." Australian Museum of
Squatting, https://web.archive.org/web/20171027115428/http://www.
australianmuseumofsquatting.org/?p=418. Accessed Sep. 9, 2024.

Nordqvist, Christian. "Wal-Mart Affects Crime Rates Negatively." *Market
Business News,* Feb. 8, 2014, https://marketbusinessnews.com/wal-mart-
affects-crime-rates-negatively/11670/.

"Nuclear Dump Would Destroy Our Land: Elder." *9News*. July 9, 2015, https://www.9news.com.au/national/elders-students-protest-sa-nuclear-dump/2c18d309-bd70-414e-b7ef-99773c032415.

Picchi, Aimee. "Union: Walmart Shut 5 Stores over Labor Activism." *CBS News*. Apr. 20, 2015, https://www.cbsnews.com/news/union-walmart-shut-5-stores-over-labor-activism/.

The Power of 504 (Full Version, Open Caption, English and Spanish). Directed by Disability Rights Education & Defense Fund, 2010. *YouTube*, https://www.youtube.com/watch?v=SyWcCuVta7M.

"Quotes." Eisenhower Presidential Library. https://www.eisenhowerlibrary.gov/eisenhowers/quotes. Accessed Sep. 11, 2024.

"Reports." National Centre for Truth and Reconciliation, University of Manitoba. Dec. 18, 2020, https://nctr.ca/records/reports/, https://nctr.ca/records/reports/.

Rose, Chris. *The Turning of the 'Spar*. Greenpeace, 1998.

Russell, Bertrand. *The Autobiography of Bertrand Russell*. George Allen & Unwin, 1969.

Schoon, Nicholas and Steve Crawshaw. "Brent Spar Affair: Two Days That Sealed Fate of Redundant Rig." *The Independent*, June 21, 1995, https://www.independent.co.uk/news/brent-spar-affair-two-days-that-sealed-fate-of-redundant-rig-1587631.html.

Schweik, Susan. "Lomax's Matrix: Disability, Solidarity, and the Black Power of 504." *Disability Studies Quarterly*, vol. 31, no. 1, Jan. 1, 2011. *www.dsq-sds.org*, https://doi.org/10.18061/dsq.v31i1.1371.

Shapiro, Joseph. "504 Sit-In: Winning Rights for the Disabled." *NPR*, Apr. 28, 2002, https://www.npr.org/2002/04/28/1142484/504-sit-in-winning-rights-for-the-disabled.

Sheehy, Gail. "Ex-Spook Sirrs: Early Osama Call Got Her Ejected." *Observer*, Mar. 15, 2004, https://observer.com/2004/03/exspook-sirrs-early-osama-call-got-her-ejected/.

Silburn, Matt. "Shawn Brant on Tyendinaga Resistance." *Rabble.ca*, Oct. 10, 2008, https://rabble.ca/general/shawn-brant-tyendinaga-resistance/.

Somal, Bharat. *India on Sale Part 2: India Plundered*. Self-published, 2015.

"Switzerland: Bomb Blast Wrecks Building on Nuclear Power Station Site." *British Pathé*, 1979, https://www.britishpathe.com/asset/134504/.

"Taliban Oil." *Al Jazeera*, https://www.aljazeera.com/program/featured-documentaries/2016/10/8/taliban-oil. Accessed Sep. 16, 2024.

Taylor, R. K. S., and Colin Pritchard. *The Protest Makers: The British Nuclear Disarmament Movement of 1958–1965, Twenty Years On.* Pergamon Press, 1980.

Teaching Heritage. Mar. 5, 2019, https://web.archive.org/web/20190305213648/http://www.teachingheritage.nsw.edu.au/section03/timeenviron.php.

Thompson, Herb. "A Most Colourful Union!" *Papers in Labour History*, no. 13, 1994: 71–89, https://web.archive.org/web/20050412224448/http://www.aucegypt.edu/faculty/thompson/herbtea/articles/blf.html.

"Time to Take Up the Fight over South Australian Nuclear Dump Plans." *Red Flag.* https://redflag.org.au/node/5556. Accessed Sep. 16, 2024.

"Transmission-Connected Generation." Independent Electricity System Operator (Ontario, Canada). https://www.ieso.ca/en/Power-Data/Supply-Overview/Transmission-Connected-Generation. Accessed Sep. 15, 2024.

Tully, John. "Green Bans and the BLF: The Labour Movement and Urban Ecology." *International Viewpoint*, Mar. 17, 2004, https://internationalviewpoint.org/spip.php?article94.

Turnipseed, Tom. "Bush, Enron, UNOCAL and the Taliban." *CounterPunch.Org*, Jan. 10, 2002, https://www.counterpunch.org/2002/01/10/bush-enron-unocal-and-the-taliban/.

"Tyendinaga Township, Land Claims Update, August 2017." https://apps.cer-rec.gc.ca/REGDOCS/Item/Open/995643.

"Walmart Closes Stores, Leaving Small Towns with No Groceries." https://web.archive.org/web/20160225061402/http://time.com/money/4192512/walmart-stores-closing-small-towns/. Accessed Sep. 15, 2024.

"Wal-Mart Loses Inglewood Referendum." https://money.cnn.com/2004/04/07/news/fortune500/walmart_inglewood/. Accessed Sep. 15, 2024.

Walter, Natasha. "How My Father Spied for Peace." *New Statesman*, May 20, 2002, https://web.archive.org/web/20171222051743/https://www.newstatesman.com/node/198271.

Ward, Colin. *Anarchy in Action*. George Allen & Unwin, Ltd., 1973. Ward's discussion of Spies for Peace archived at https://anarchyinaction.org/index.php?title=Spies_for_Peace.

"Waste Management Revenue 2010–2024." https://www.macrotrends.net/stocks/charts/WM/waste-management/revenue. Accessed Sep. 18, 2024.

"'We Shall Not Be Moved' The 504 Sit-In for Disability Civil Rights." Disability Rights Education & Defense Fund (DREDF), June 1, 1997, https://dredf.org/we-shall-not-be-moved/.

Wolfe, S. E., and D. C. Pyrooz. "Rolling Back Prices and Raising Crime Rates? The Walmart Effect on Crime in the United States." *British Journal of Criminology*, vol. 54, no. 2, Mar. 2014, pp. 199–221, (cross-reference) https://doi.org/10.1093/bjc/azt071.

Wolff-Mann, Ethan. "The New Way That Walmart Is Ruining America's Small Towns." *Money.com*, Feb. 25, 2016, https://web.archive.org/web/20160128012201/http://time.com/money/4192512/walmart-stores-closing-small-towns/.

Worsnop, Tom, and Maz Kerin. "Taking Roxby to Town." *Chain Reaction*, vol. 1, no. 40, Jan. 1985, https://www.reasoninrevolt.net.au/objects/pdf/d1097.pdf.

NOTES

1. Indigenous Environmental Network, 2021.
2. Canadian National Rail layoffs will "further complicate" tangled supply chain, 2020.
3. You can read more about Cabral, and his movement-building and recruitment skills, in chapter 4 of *Full Spectrum Resistance*.
4. Cabral, *Revolution in Guinea*, pp. 70–72.
5. Government of Canada, "Statement of Apology to Former Students of Indian Residential Schools."
6. "Reports." National Centre for Truth and Reconciliation, 2020.
7. For detailed exploration of these policies, and Macdonald's role in them, see the excellent book *Clearing the Plains* by James Daschuk.
8. Andre Henry, personal Facebook post, January 7, 2024.
9. This a topic that adrienne maree brown has written brilliantly about in books like *We Will Not Cancel Us*.
10. Some of my "selection bias" in this book is that I want to be relevant to the people I mostly work with. Organizing in a settler-colonial country like Canada, the US, or Australia, is different from organizing in a "post-colonial" country like India or Nigeria. My audience, my experience, and my comrades are mostly in English-speaking countries in the Global North. This is not an academic survey, but a practical book meant to be of direct and immediate use to organizing communities I already know, so I have chosen to emphasize stories from more "transferable" geographic areas.
11. See *Full Spectrum Resistance*, chapter 4: Recruitment and Retention.
12. Burgmann, *Power and Protest*.
13. Consider this quote from a BLF member: "If I was asked prior to the 1970 strike what I did for a living, I'd probably mumble, 'Oh, I'm a builder's labourer." After that, if somebody asked me what I did for a living, I was a bloody BL!" 1970s: Victoria St Squats.
14. Burgmann, *Power and Protest*, and Teaching Heritage.
15. New Matilda, "Green Bans That Saved Sydney."
16. Ibid.
17. Teaching Heritage.
18. "Man Behind the Pink Ban."
19. Tully, "Green Bans and the BLF."
20. Teaching Heritage.
21. Mundey, *Green Bans and Beyond*, 148.
22. Economics professor Herb Thompson argued that Gallagher's "oft-quoted Maoist pronouncements, revolutionary rhetoric and self-styled antagonism towards the State were spurious. Norm Gallagher saw his function as a union official to be an operative within the constraints of capitalism, not in opposition to it." The BLF of New South Wales, on the other hand, were "more ingenious in portraying unionism as working class institutions in opposition to capitalism as an exploitative social formation." Thompson, "A Most Colourful Union."
23. Burgmann and Burgmann, *Green Bans, Red Union*, 54. Democratic and grassroots unions can be powerful forces for justice. But undemocratic centralized unions can be no different from any other unaccountable power, be it a government or a corporation. While anarchists and socialists in the labour movement of the time were often

     connected with grassroots militancy, Maoists—perhaps because of their authoritarian tendencies—were prone to side with bosses in some of these disagreements.

24. Caroline Graham, "Life and Times of Juanita Nielsen, 2007."
25. Ibid.
26. "1970s: Victoria St Squats."
27. Nielsen was wealthy but—like the women suburbanites of the first green ban—she was able to work effectively with working class allies.
28. Teaching Heritage.
29. Calculated from Teaching Heritage.
30. The proponents of neoliberal austerity, who work to dismantle unions and undermine the social safety net, intentionally keep people in precarious economic situations to make it harder for working people to resist.
31. Mundey, *Green Bans and Beyond*, 148.
32. Burgmann and Burgmann, *Green Bans, Red Union*, 9–10.
33. Leong, "Struggle over Parcel C," 2. This gives it a population density of 111 people per acre—on par with Mumbai, India.
34. Ibid.
35. Ibid.
36. Ibid, 2.
37. Ibid.
38. Leong, "Struggle over Parcel C," 3.
39. That designation emerged in part from a 1986 community campaign about Parcel C.
40. Leong, "Struggle over Parcel C," 6.
41. Ibid, 8.
42. Ibid, 10.
43. Ibid, 9.
44. Lai et al., "Lessons of the Parcel C Struggle."
45. Leong, "Struggle over Parcel C," 12–13. Emphasis added.
46. Cone, "Short History of the 504 Sit-in."
47. Dawson, "Ed Roberts' Wheelchair Records a Story of Obstacles Overcome | Smithsonian."
48. "We Shall Not Be Moved," DREDF.
49. Cone, "Short History of the 504 Sit-in."
50. "We Shall Not Be Moved," DREDF.
51. Disability Rights Education and Defense Fund, "The Power of 504," 2008.
52. Cone, "Short History of the 504 Sit-in."
53. Cone, "Short History of the 504 Sit-in."
54. Shapiro, 2002.
55. Lauby, 2015.
56. "We Shall Not Be Moved," DREDF.
57. Cone, "Short History of the 504 Sit-in."
58. "We Shall Not Be Moved," DREDF. Note that Rosewater used the number of 28 million; news reports at the time also gave the higher number of 35 million people benefiting.
59. Cone, "Short History of the 504 Sit-in."
60. "We Shall Not Be Moved," DREDF.
61. Cone, "Short History of the 504 Sit-in."
62. Cone, "Short History of the 504 Sit-in."
63. Disability Rights Education and Defense Fund, "The Power of 504", 2008.
64. Lauby, 2015.

65. Schweik, 2011.
66. "We Shall Not Be Moved," DREDF.
67. "We Shall Not Be Moved," DREDF.
68. Cone, "Short History of the 504 Sit-in."
69. Ibid.
70. Ibid.
71. "The Power of 504" documentary calls the sit-ins "spontaneous" and that is possibly how it looked from the outside. But organizers had been planning and laying the groundwork for years, and coordinating across the US.
72. Blum, *Killing Hope.*
73. Rose, *Turning of the 'Spar,* 9.
74. Ibid, 19.
75. Guyon, Why is the world's most profitable company.
76. Specifically, the "Statue" part of the Statue of Liberty is 46 metres high. From the top of the torch to ground level (including the pedestal and foundation) is a distance of 93 metres.
77. Rose, *Turning of the 'Spar,* 30.
78. Ibid, 24–26, p. 42.
79. Ibid, 61.
80. Ibid, 10, p. 33.
81. Ibid, 9.
82. Ibid.
83. Ibid.
84. Ibid, 11.
85. Ibid, 113.
86. Ibid, 102.
87. Ibid.
88. Ibid, 103 and p. 122: "From Sweden, Environment Minister Anna Lind said: 'Marvellous—this shows it's worth protesting." In Germany, Environment Minister Angela Merkel declared herself 'delighted.'"
89. Ibid, 103.
90. Ibid, 110.
91. Ibid, 122.
92. Ibid, 127.
93. Ibid, 129.
94. Ibid.
95. Ibid, 130.
96. Schoon and Crawshaw, "Brent Spar Affair."
97. Rose, *Turning of the 'Spar,* 24.
98. The final announcement on the fate of the structure was not made until January 29, 1998.
99. Rose, *Turning of the 'Spar,* 102.
100. Duff, *Left, Left, Left,* 116.
101. Ibid, 221.
102. Ibid, 125.
103. Ibid, 130.
104. Ibid, 167.
105. Ibid.
106. Ibid.
107. Ibid.

108. Ibid, 167–168.
109. Ibid, 168.
110. Ibid.
111. Ibid, 169.
112. Ibid, 169–170. See, in particular, the protest at Harrington with separate groups for civil disobedience and the CND mainstream.
113. Carroll, "Danger! Official Secret," 6.
114. Carroll, "Danger! Official Secret," 6.
115. Duff, *Left, Left, Left*, 2011, 181.
116. Russell, 1969, 113.
117. Carroll, "Danger! Official Secret," 129.
118. Carroll, "Danger! Official Secret," 134.
119. Walter, "How my father spied for peace."
120. Duff, *Left, Left, Left*, 220.
121. Taylor and Pritchard, *Protest Makers*.
122. Quotes, Eisenhower Presidential Library.
123. I want to express my gratitude to Dr. Carroll for her insightful and comprehensive analyses of the nuclear disarmament movements discussed here. I owe a lot to her research, and I'm also grateful that she took the time to retrieve and scan some historical documents from her own archive to share with me when I prepared this chapter.
124. Carroll, "Danger! Official Secret," 157.
125. Carroll, "Danger! Official Secret," 9.
126. Duff, *Left, Left, Left*, 154.
127. Ibid.
128. Brewood et al., "Beyond Counting Arses," 1.
129. Brewood et al., "Beyond Counting Arses," 2.
130. Carroll, "Danger! Official Secret," 187.
131. Brewood et al., "Beyond Counting Arses," 2.
132. Brewood et al., "Beyond Counting Arses," 3.
133. Ibid.
134. Ibid.
135. Ibid.
136. Ibid.
137. Ward, *Anarchy in Action*.
138. Carroll, "Danger! Official Secret," 141.
139. Carroll, "Danger! Official Secret," 142–3.
140. Brewood et al., "Beyond Counting Arses," 1.
141. Brewood et al., "Beyond Counting Arses," 1.
142. Brewood et al., "Beyond Counting Arses," 5.
143. Brewood et al., "Beyond Counting Arses," 5–6.
144. Brewood et al., "Beyond Counting Arses," 6.
145. Duff, *Left, Left, Left*, 131.
146. Ibid, 224.
147. Ibid, emphasis added.
148. Brewood et al., "Beyond Counting Arses," 6.
149. Ibid, 7.
150. Carroll, "Danger! Official Secret," 120-121.
151. Mossman, 1975.
152. Ibid.

153. Schils, 2011.
154. Mossman, 1975.
155. Ibid.
156. Schils, 2011.
157. Milder, 2013.
158. Milder, 2012, 194
159. Ibid, 195.
160. Ibid, 198.
161. Wolfgang Rüdig (1990). *Anti-Nuclear Movements: A World Survey of Opposition to Nuclear Energy*, Longman, 135.
162. Ibid, 216.
163. Schils, 2011.
164. Engels, "Gender Roles and German Anti-Nuclear Protest," 410.
165. Ibid, 416.
166. Ibid, 414.
167. Milder, *Greening Democracy*, 256, citing "Wieder ein Ostermarsch – Wyhl," *Infodienst*.
168. Milder, 2012, 279.
169. Ibid.
170. https://journals.sagepub.com/doi/full/10.1177/0096340212464357.
171. "Switzerland: Bomb blast wrecks building on nuclear power station site."
172. *Bulletin of the Atomic Scientists*, "Renewable Wackersdorf," 7.
173. Milder, 2013.
174. "Europe's Heatwave Is Forcing Nuclear Power Plants to Shut Down."
175. "Emu Field," *Australian Nuclear and Uranium Sites*.
176. "Maralinga Nuclear Tests 60 Years on: What Do We Know Now?"
177. Cross and Hudson, *Beyond Belief*, 23–25.
178. "Time to Take Up the Fight over South Australian Nuclear Dump Plans."
179. "Nuclear Dump Would Destroy Our Land: Elder."
180. Beaton and Green, *Standing Strong*.
181. Worsnop and Kerin, "Taking Roxby to Town."
182. Malekar, "Fish Wars in the Global South."
183. Ibid.
184. For background, see: Sheehy, "Ex-Spook Sirrs"; Turnipseed, "Bush, Enron, UNOCAL."; "Taliban Oil"; and "Afghanistan: It's About Oil."
185. Somal, *India on Sale*.
186. Semwal, 27.
187. Ibid, 8.
188. Ibid, 28.
189. Ibid.
190. Ibid, 2.
191. Malekar, "Fish Wars in the Global South."
192. For analysis, see "Another Network is Possible".
193. Buildup along Line 9 in Toronto without emergency plans being set.
194. What's another $4 billion among friends?
195. "Transmission-Connected Generation."
196. Personal correspondence with the National Observer.
197. Waste Management Revenue 2010–2024.
198. Forkert, *Fighting Dirty*, 25.
199. Ibid, 30.
200. Ibid, 36.

201. Ibid, 70.
202. Ibid, 97–99.
203. Ibid, 116.
204. Ibid, 94.
205. Ibid, 68.
206. Shawn Brant on Tyendinaga resistance, Silburn, 2008.
207. CN Rail layoffs will 'further complicate' tangled supply chain. Tyendinaga is located near the midpoint of the Quebec City–Windsor rail corridor, which is also the busiest passenger rail corridor in Canada.
208. Tyendinaga Township, Land Claims Update, August 2017.
209. Forkert, *Fighting Dirty*, 94.
210. Ibid, 93.
211. Ibid, 47.
212. Ibid, 153.
213. Ibid, 155.
214. Ibid, 45. Forkert notes that Allan Gardiner told her: "Those were early days . . . and we had no idea then how much worse it could get . . . We could not possibly have imagined the ensuring nightmare or that the dump issue would consume our lives for such a long time—decades, it turned out."
215. Ibid, 38.
216. Ibid, 134.
217. Ibid, 136.
218. Ibid, 156.
219. Ibid, 65.
220. Ibid, 45.
221. By which I mean: Canada wouldn't exist if it hadn't stolen huge amounts of land from Indigenous peoples, and Canada's behavior toward Indigenous peoples has been consistently horrendous.
222. Minister signs deal to return land to Tyendinaga Mohawk Territory.
223. Forkert, *Fighting Dirty*, 116.
224. Ibid, 155.
225. Ibid, 41.
226. Ibid, 154–155.
227. Ibid, 7.
228. Ibid, 65.
229. Ibid, 21.
230. Ibid, 8.
231. Ibid, 48–59.
232. Ibid, 49.
233. Baines, "Wal-Mart's Power Trajectory."
234. See: Heilemann, "Why Wal-Mart Wants to Invade New York"; "Wal-Mart loses Inglewood Referendum"; Greenhouse and Clifford, "A Respite in Efforts by Wal-Mart in New York", and Boccaccio, "Walmart blocked from entering New York City."
235. "Wal-Mart and County-Wide Poverty."
236. Neumark, David, et al. "The Effects of Wal-Mart on Local Labor Markets."
237. Wal-Mart affects crime rates negatively. "Lead author of the study, titled 'Rolling back prices and raising crime rates? The Wal-Mart effect on crime in the United States,' Scott Wolfe, assistant professor of criminology and criminal justice, said: 'The crime decline was stunted in counties where Wal-Mart expanded in the 1990s. If the corporation built a new store, there were 17 additional property crimes and 2 additional violent

crimes for every 10,000 persons in a county.'" See Wolfe and Pyrooz, "Rolling Back Prices and Raising Crime Rates? The Walmart Effect on Crime in the United States."
238. "Wal-Mart and County-Wide Poverty."
239. See Miller, Miller, Ken. "Small-Town Budgets Hurting from Loss of Mini Walmarts" and "Walmart Closes Stores, Leaving Small Towns with No Groceries."
240. Lichtenstein "Wal-Mart Tries to Go to Town."
241. These community efforts combined with external challenges that Walmart faced at the time, as Al Norman described in his October 2007 article, "Hey, We Cut Wal-Mart in Half!" Shortly after that article was published, the Great Recession began, another hit for Walmart.
242. Baines, "Wal-Mart's Power Trajectory."
243. Clifford, "Walmart Strains to Keep Aisles Stocked Fresh."
244. About 23,000 of which would have been converted to Walmart jobs, and roughly 10,000 of which would have been eliminated completely.
245. Bose, "Half of Walmart's Workforce Are Part-time Workers: Labour Group."
246. Picchi, "Union: Walmart Shut 5 Stores over Labor Activism."
247. "How Walmart Keeps an Eye on Its Massive Workforce."
248. "Labor Groups Are Taking On Walmart And McDonald's. But Who Will Fund Their Fight?"
249. Bank Muñoz, *Building Power from Below*, 2.
250. Ibid, 2.
251. Ibid, 2.
252. Ibid, 16.
253. Ibid, 12–13.
254. Ibid, 17.
255. Ibid, 20.
256. Ibid, 83–84.
257. Ibid, 20.
258. Ibid, 2.

INDEX